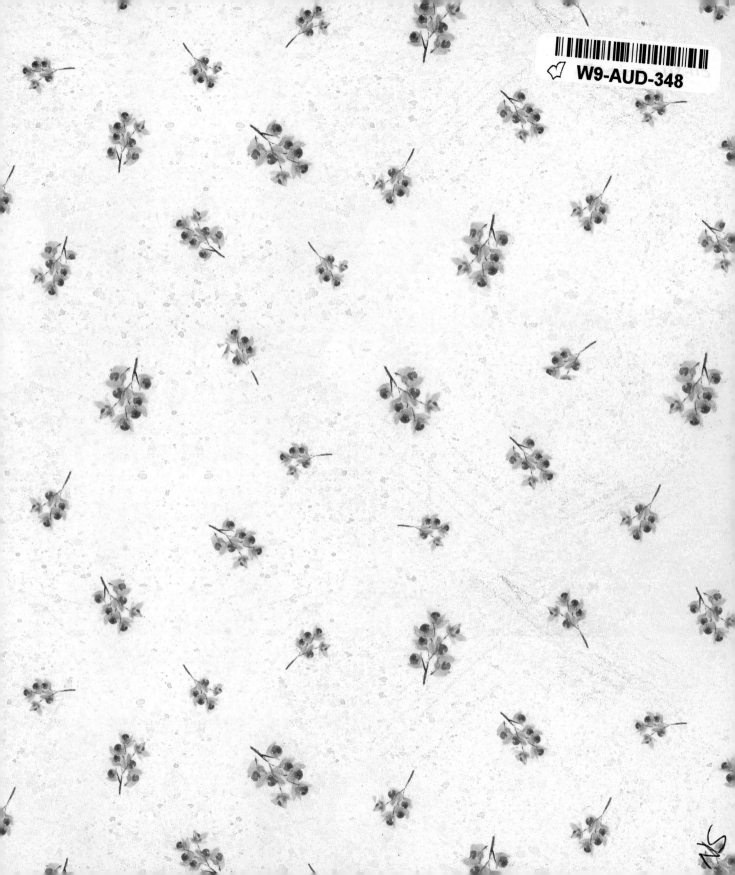

coming
home
WITH GOOSEBERRY PATCH

This book is dedicated to our families...forever in our hearts, their love and support are with us every day. Also, to dear friends, old and new...thank you for welcoming us into your lives and sharing your homes with us.

1-800-854-6673
www.gooseberrypatch.com

Vickie & JoAnn

THE GOOSEBERRY PATCH STORY

There are so many joys of living in a small town…Saturday morning farmers' markets, barn auctions, spirited parades down the main street and Friday night football games. Friends wave as you drive by and neighbors catch up over the backyard fence.

As friends and neighbors we spent time chatting about our kids, the latest flea market or an upcoming barn sale. We loved vintage finds and painted furniture…anything old and country-style.

After a walk home in the fall of 1984, we began to talk about how much we'd love working from home to be with our families, and it wasn't long after that when we sat down at the kitchen table for the first of many brainstorming sessions. It was then we created our very first catalog! We filled it with quilts, baskets, handmade cookie cutters, candles and wreaths. Before we knew it, we began hearing from others who shared the same heartfelt connection to the country lifestyle. Soon they began to share their treasured family recipes and sweet memories. We combined them with whimsical illustrations and created our first cookbook called *Old-Fashioned Country Christmas*. Since then, we've created over 50 community-style cookbooks.

Our second full-color book, *Coming Home with Gooseberry Patch*, celebrates the times we spend with family, friends and neighbors. And whether it's a picnic, bake sale, Halloween get-together, Thanksgiving or Christmas gathering, we hope you'll find new recipes, fresh decorating ideas and inspiration to make memories that last.

Welcome Home!
Vickie & JoAnn

contents

it's *halloween*

Italian Sausage & Vegetable Soup

Crunchy Hot Chicken Salad

Glowing pumpkins on every porch and rustling leaves in every corner. An autumn sunset, glinting through bare branches, gives way to a golden harvest moon. Cobwebs in doorways, old rockers creaking on the porch and flickering candlelight combine with vintage-inspired decorations to set an eerie mood. It's the end of October and time to conjure up some magic!

Make the evening bewitching...pumpkin party bags are simple to make and so are delightful Chocolate-Dipped Spoons. We'll even show you a whole new twist on bobbing for apples... tempting glazed doughnuts dangling from tree branches just waiting to be caught!

You won't have to carve out much time on the menu either...everything is quick & easy. Mummy Hot Dogs will make little ones giggle and A Great Pumpkin Cheese Ball has a flavorful combination of both sharp Cheddar and blue cheeses. Finally, take the evening chill off with mugs of spiced Pumpkin Latté. So go ahead, Halloween only comes once a year, scare up a few friends for treats and fun!

A Great Pumpkin Cheese Ball

We added a stem from a real mini pumpkin! Just snap off a stem, rinse and insert into the top of the cheese ball.

8-oz. pkg. cream cheese, softened
10-oz. container sharp Cheddar
    cold-pack cheese spread
1/4 c. crumbled blue cheese
2 t. Worcestershire sauce
1/4 t. celery salt
1/4 t. onion salt
1/2 c. walnuts, finely chopped
1 t. paprika
Garnish: 1 pretzel rod, broken in half,
    assorted crackers

Blend together cheeses until smooth. Stir in Worcestershire sauce, celery salt and onion salt, adding more to taste if desired. Shape into a ball and set on serving plate; cover and chill for 2 to 3 hours, until firm. If desired, score vertical lines with a knife to resemble a pumpkin. Toss walnuts with paprika; press into surface of cheese ball. Break pretzel rod in half and insert in top for stem. Arrange crackers around cheese ball. Makes 10 to 12 servings.

Sweet Onion & Zucchini Bake

Create a costume in no time using a plain party-store mask. Replace the elastic with shimmering ribbon, then cover the mask with paper or fabric flowers and petals, pressed leaves, even feathers. Craft glue will hold them in place and you'll have a one-of-a-kind creation.

A Great Pumpkin Cheese Ball

Crunchy Hot Chicken Salad

This fantastic favorite is surprisingly simple to prepare.

6 T. butter, divided
1 c. celery, chopped
1/2 c. green pepper, diced
1/3 c. onion, chopped
2 to 3 T. pimentos, diced
4-oz. can sliced mushrooms, drained
2-1/4 oz. pkg. slivered almonds
4 c. cooked chicken, diced
1 c. mayonnaise
10-3/4 oz. can cream of celery soup
1 t. salt
1 c. corn flake cereal, crushed

Melt 4 tablespoons butter in a large skillet over medium heat; add vegetables and almonds. Sauté until vegetables are tender; spoon into an ungreased 13"x9" baking pan. Add chicken, mayonnaise, soup and salt; mix well. Melt remaining butter and toss with cereal; sprinkle over top. Bake at 350 degrees for 30 minutes. Makes 10 servings.

Sweet Onion & Zucchini Bake

You'll be amazed at how delicious this is!

1/4 c. butter
3 c. sweet onion, thinly sliced
3 c. zucchini, thinly sliced
2 eggs, beaten
1/4 c. half-and-half
1 t. salt
1/8 t. pepper
1/4 t. dry mustard
1 c. Swiss cheese, shredded
   and divided

Melt butter in a large skillet over medium heat; sauté onion and zucchini until tender. Arrange vegetables in a lightly greased 8"x8" baking pan. Combine eggs, half-and-half, salt, pepper, mustard and 1/2 cup cheese. Pour egg mixture over vegetables; sprinkle with remaining cheese. Bake at 375 degrees for 20 minutes, or until center is set. Makes 6 to 8 servings.

Italian Sausage & Vegetable Soup

A great make-ahead soup recipe...even more flavorful when you reheat it.

1/2 lb. ground Italian pork sausage
1 onion, finely chopped
1 clove garlic, minced
3 14-oz. cans chicken broth
1/2 c. white wine or chicken broth
28-oz. can crushed tomatoes in
    tomato purée
2 zucchini, quartered lengthwise
    and sliced
2 carrots, peeled and diced
3 stalks celery, diced
1 green pepper, diced
1 t. dried basil
1/2 t. dried oregano
1/2 c. orzo pasta, uncooked
1/2 t. salt
1/2 t. pepper
Optional: 2/3 c. shredded Parmesan
    cheese

Brown sausage in a Dutch oven over medium heat. Drain, leaving a small amount of drippings in pan. Add onion and garlic; cook just until tender. Add broth, wine or broth, vegetables and seasonings; bring to a boil. Add uncooked pasta; reduce heat and simmer for 20 minutes, until vegetables and pasta are tender. Add salt and pepper to taste. Sprinkle servings with Parmesan cheese, if desired. Makes 6 to 8 servings.

Instead of using a big hollowed-out pumpkin as a soup tureen, turn smaller sugar pumpkins into individual soup bowls. Hollow out several, fill each with soup and replace the pumpkin "lid" to keep soup warm. Set several on a platter surrounded with real pumpkin leaves and curly vines.

Mummy Hot Dogs

Hot dogs with a Halloween twist!

11-oz. tube refrigerated bread stick
   dough
12 hot dogs
1 egg
1 T. water
Garnish: mustard

Separate dough into strips. Wrap one
strip of dough around each hot dog,
leaving 1/2 inch uncovered for face.
Arrange on a lightly greased baking
sheet. Whisk together egg and water;
brush over dough. Bake at 350 degrees
for 14 to 16 minutes, until golden. Dot
mustard on hot dogs with a toothpick
to form eyes. Makes 12 servings.

Chocolate-Dipped Spoons

*Stir a little sweetness into mugs of
steaming cocoa.*

12-oz. pkg. semi-sweet chocolate chips
2 t. shortening
35 to 45 plastic spoons
Garnish: candies for decorating

Line baking sheets with parchment
paper; set aside. Place chocolate chips
in a microwave-safe bowl; microwave
on medium power for 2 minutes, or
until melted, stirring every 30 seconds.
To thin chocolate, add shortening to
chocolate; stir gently. Dip each plastic
spoon into chocolate mixture to cover
the bowl of the spoon; place on
parchment paper to set. Arrange
candies on spoons as desired while
chocolate is still soft; cool thoroughly.
Makes 35 to 45 spoons.

*Chocolate-Dipped Spoons
and Pumpkin Latté*

Pumpkin Latté

A scrumptious way to warm up on a brisk autumn day.

4 c. milk
4 T. canned pumpkin
3 T. vanilla extract
1 t. cinnamon
2 c. strong, hot brewed coffee
Garnish: whipped cream, pumpkin
    pie spice, cinnamon sticks

Stir together milk and pumpkin in a
saucepan; heat over low heat until
steaming. Stir in vanilla and cinnamon.
With a hand-held blender or electric
mixer, blend for 15 to 20 seconds, until
thick and foamy. Pour into 4 to 6 mugs
or tall glasses; pour in hot coffee. Top
with whipped cream; sprinkle with
spice and add cinnamon stick stirrers.
Serve immediately. Makes 4 servings.

Frothy Orange Punch

The orange flavor is so refreshing...kids big & little will love this.

2 pts. vanilla ice cream, softened
2 pts. orange sherbet, softened
4 c. milk
2 c. orange soda, chilled

Scoop ice cream and sherbet into a
punch bowl. Pour in milk and soda;
stir gently. Serve immediately. Makes
15 to 20 servings.

Mummy Hot Dogs

Spiced Pumpkin Bread

Spiced Pumpkin Bread

A fun autumn treat to share with friends and neighbors.

2 c. canned pumpkin
3 c. sugar
1 c. water
1 c. oil
4 eggs
3-1/3 c. all-purpose flour
2 t. baking soda
1 t. baking powder
1 t. salt
2 t. cinnamon
3/4 t. ground cloves
1/2 t. nutmeg

Combine pumpkin, sugar, water, oil and eggs in a large bowl; beat until well mixed. Set aside. Stir together remaining ingredients in another bowl; slowly add to pumpkin mixture, beating until smooth. Grease and flour two, 9"x5" loaf pans or six, 5-1/2"x3" mini loaf pans; divide batter between pans. Bake at 350 degrees for 60 to 65 minutes for regular loaves or 50 to 55 minutes for mini loaves, until a toothpick inserted in center tests clean. Let cool in pans for 10 to 15 minutes; invert bread onto a wire rack to finish cooling. Makes 2 loaves or 6 mini loaves.

Pumpkin Ice Cream

As yummy as pumpkin pie...without the crust! Freeze in a 13"x9" pan, and use Halloween cookie cutters to make individual servings.

1/2 gal. vanilla ice cream, softened
1 c. canned pumpkin
1/2 c. brown sugar, packed
1/2 t. ground ginger
1/4 t. cinnamon
1/4 t. nutmeg
1 T. orange juice

Place ice cream in a large bowl; set aside. Mix remaining ingredients with an electric mixer on low speed; blend into ice cream. Cover; freeze. Let soften slightly before scooping for serving. Makes 8 to 10 servings.

Crepe paper pumpkin party bags are easy to make and fill with Nutty Popcorn Snack Mix. Cut a 12-inch circle from orange crepe paper, then place snack mix in the center. Draw together the paper above the mix and twist to close. Secure the bag with green florist's tape wrapped around the twist to create a stem.

Spooky Spiderweb Cupcakes

Don't worry about making the "webs" perfect...the more imperfect, the spookier the effect.

18-1/4 oz. pkg. chocolate or spice cake mix
1/2 c. semi-sweet chocolate chips
16-oz. container vanilla or orange frosting

Prepare cake mix according to package directions. Bake in 18 to 24 paper-lined muffin cups. Cool and set aside. Place chocolate chips in a small plastic zipping bag; microwave on high setting for 30 seconds to one minute, until melted. Snip off one corner of bag to form a small hole; squeeze chocolate onto a wax paper-lined baking sheet to form 3 concentric circles. Immediately draw a toothpick through circles to form spiderweb design. Repeat with remaining chocolate; chill until set. Frost cupcakes; press webs gently into frosting. Makes 18 to 24 cupcakes.

Spooky Spiderweb Cupcakes

Pumpkin Ice Cream

18

Black Cat Cut-Out Cookies

Fun for goblins of all ages to make!

1 c. butter, softened
2/3 c. sugar
1 egg
1 t. vanilla extract
2-1/2 c. all-purpose flour
Garnish: black sanding sugar, small
   candies (for eyes)

Blend together butter and sugar; stir in egg and vanilla. Add flour; mix until well blended. Shape into a ball; cover and chill for 4 hours to overnight. Roll out dough 1/4-inch thick on a lightly floured surface; cut out with cookie cutters as desired. Arrange cookies on lightly greased baking sheets; bake at 350 degrees for 8 to 10 minutes, or until golden. Frost cookies when cool; sprinkle with black sanding sugar and add candy "eyes." Makes about 2 dozen.

Chocolate Frosting:

2-1/4 c. powdered sugar
3 T. butter, melted
3 T. milk
1 T. vanilla extract
1-1/2 t. lemon juice
2 to 3 T. baking cocoa

Combine all ingredients in a medium bowl. Beat with an electric mixer on low speed until smooth.

Be sure to set a treat table at your Halloween get-together. Fill vintage-style painted metal pails with cello bags of cookies and candies. For a fun twist, cinch each bag closed with a black licorice whip.

Nutty Popcorn Snack Mix

If you're using microwave popcorn, simply pop two, 3-1/2 oz. packages.

16 c. popped popcorn
5 c. mini pretzel twists
2 c. brown sugar, packed
1 c. margarine
1/2 c. dark corn syrup
1/2 t. salt
1/2 t. baking soda
1 t. vanilla extract
1 c. dry-roasted peanuts
2 c. candy corn or candy-coated
    chocolates

Combine popcorn and pretzels in a large roasting pan; set aside. Combine brown sugar, margarine, corn syrup and salt in a heavy medium saucepan. Cook over medium heat for 12 to 14 minutes, stirring occasionally, until mixture comes to a full boil. Continue cooking and stirring for 4 to 6 minutes, until mixture reaches the soft-ball stage, or 234 to 243 degrees on a candy thermometer. Remove from heat; stir in baking soda and vanilla. Pour over popcorn and pretzels in roasting pan; sprinkle in peanuts. Stir until popcorn mixture is coated well. Bake at 200 degrees for 20 minutes; stir. Bake for an additional 25 minutes. Remove from oven; stir in candy. Immediately spoon onto wax paper; let cool completely. Break into pieces; store in an airtight container. Makes about 24 cups.

Nutty Popcorn Snack Mix

giving *thanks*

Wild Mushroom & Thyme Spoon Bread

Coming home...

if there is one day each year when food and family come together, it's Thanksgiving. At the heart of the day are tradition, comfort and a longing for simpler times. We visit friends & family, watch parades and football, and eagerly anticipate favorite foods that are only brought out for this special day.

Expected Thanksgiving favorites can take a tasty twist... Cranberry-Apple Glazed Turkey, Savory Cheese & Bacon Potatoes and Sweet Potato Praline Casserole. Sample scrumptious new additions to your bountiful holiday table such as Wild Mushroom & Thyme Spoon Bread, Marbled Pumpkin Cheesecake and Mom's Apple-Cranberry Pie.

And the day after Thanksgiving means more than just turkey sandwiches! Surprise your family with Golden Shepherd's Pie or Tangy Turkey Cobb Salad topped with a flavorful cranberry vinaigrette.

Slow down and enjoy. Thanksgiving is a day spent with family & friends...savor every moment.

Crunchy Apple-Pear Salad

*Toss together green Granny Smith apples
with red Anjou and yellow Bartlett pears
in this recipe...so colorful!*

2 apples, cored and cubed
2 pears, cored and thinly sliced
1 T. lemon juice
2 heads butter lettuce, torn
    into bite-size pieces
1/2 c. crumbled gorgonzola cheese
1/2 c. chopped walnuts, toasted

Toss apples and pears with lemon
juice; drain. Arrange lettuce on 6 salad
plates; top with apples, pears and
gorgonzola cheese. Drizzle salad with
dressing; sprinkle with walnuts. Serve
immediately. Makes 6 servings.

Dressing:

1 c. oil
6 T. cider vinegar
1/2 c. sugar
1 t. celery seed
1/2 t. salt
1/4 t. pepper

Combine ingredients in a jar with a
tight-fitting lid; cover. Shake well until
dressing is blended and sugar dissolves.
Keep refrigerated.

Savory Cheese & Bacon Potatoes

*Cheesy potatoes that are likely to become
a must-have at any gathering.*

2-1/2 lbs. Yukon Gold potatoes, peeled
    and quartered
3 T. butter, softened
2-1/2 c. mixed shredded cheese blend
    (such as Swiss, Italian and/or
    casserole style)
1/2 to 3/4 c. milk, warmed
4 slices bacon, crisply cooked and
    crumbled
2 t. dried sage
salt and pepper to taste
Optional: additional shredded cheese

Cover potatoes with water in a large
saucepan. Bring to a boil; cook until
tender, 15 to 18 minutes. Drain
potatoes; place in a large bowl and
mash. Blend in butter and cheese; add
milk to make a creamy consistency. Stir
in bacon and sage; add salt and pepper
to taste. Sprinkle with additional
cheese, if desired. Makes 8 servings.

Thanks

Wild Mushroom & Thyme Spoon Bread

You'll love this dressed-up southern favorite.

2 T. oil, divided
1 onion, chopped
2 cloves garlic, minced
1 T. fresh thyme, minced
4-oz. pkg. cremini mushrooms, sliced
4-oz. pkg. shiitake mushrooms, sliced
2 c. chicken broth
1 t. seasoned salt
1 c. cornmeal
1 c. milk
4 eggs, separated
Optional: fresh thyme sprigs

Heat one tablespoon oil in a large skillet over medium-high heat. Add onion, garlic and thyme; sauté until softened, 3 to 5 minutes. Set aside. Reduce heat to low; add remaining oil and mushrooms to skillet. Cover and cook until liquid evaporates, about 8 minutes, stirring occasionally. Stir in onion mixture, reserving 1/2 cup mixture for topping. In a saucepan over high heat, bring broth and salt to a boil. Gradually add cornmeal, whisking well; cook and stir for one minute. Remove from heat; stir in mushroom mixture, milk and egg yolks. Beat egg whites until stiff with an electric mixer on high speed; gently fold into cornmeal mixture. Pour into a 2-quart casserole dish that has been sprayed with non-stick vegetable spray. Bake at 400 degrees for 35 to 40 minutes, until puffy and set. Warm reserved mushroom mixture; spoon over top. Garnish with fresh thyme sprigs, if desired. Makes 8 servings.

Pastry leaves look so pretty on the edges of our Marbled Pumpkin Cheesecake. Simply dip mini cookie cutters in flour and cut out shapes from a ready-made pie crust. Lightly brush the "leaves" with water, sprinkle with sugar and bake at 350 degrees until golden. Arrange cooled leaves around the rim of the cheesecake. For festive color, coat fresh cranberries with corn syrup, roll in sugar and place among the "leaves."

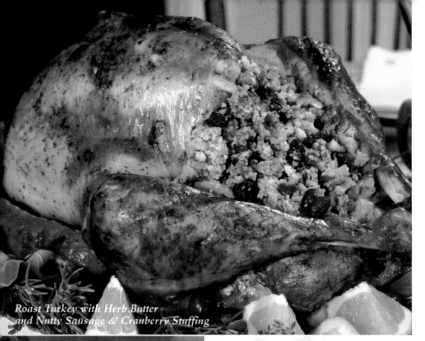
Roast Turkey with Herb Butter and Nutty Sausage & Cranberry Stuffing

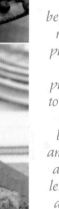
Farmhouse Apple Bread

You'll be the talk of the town with this Thanksgiving welcome! Several weeks before your pumpkin patch is ready to harvest, choose a pumpkin that's deep orange in color. Don't pick the pumpkin...it has to continue to grow in the patch. Simply wipe it clean with a mild bleach and water solution and use a craft knife to write a greeting on the shell...the letters should only be carved about 1/8-inch deep. Now wipe the pumpkin clean again, and as the pumpkin grows, so will your message.

Sweet Potato Praline Casserole

A fall favorite that is simple to prepare.

3 15-oz. cans sweet potatoes, drained
2 eggs, beaten
1/2 c. milk
1/3 c. sugar
5 T. butter, melted and divided
2 T. frozen orange juice
    concentrate, thawed
1/2 t. salt
2/3 c. chopped pecans
1/3 c. brown sugar, packed
2 T. all-purpose flour
Optional: 1-1/2 c. mini
    marshmallows

Mash sweet potatoes; add eggs, milk, sugar, 3 tablespoons melted butter, orange juice and salt. Mix until smooth. Spread in a greased 2-quart casserole dish; set aside. Stir together pecans, brown sugar, flour and remaining butter in a small bowl; sprinkle evenly over sweet potato mixture. Bake, uncovered, at 350 degrees for 30 to 40 minutes. If desired, remove from oven after 30 minutes; sprinkle with marshmallows and bake an additional 5 to 10 minutes, until golden. Let stand 5 minutes before serving. Makes 8 to 10 servings.

Roast Turkey with Herb Butter

giving

You'll find this turkey is tender, moist and flavorful. Serve the remaining herb butter spread on warm dinner rolls.

12 to 14-lb. turkey
6 T. Herb Butter, softened and divided
1 T. salt
1 t. pepper
1 onion, quartered
4 stalks celery, chopped
1 lemon, quartered

Rinse turkey and pat dry. Set aside giblets, reserving for broth if desired. Place turkey in a roasting pan. Gently loosen skin on breast; spread one tablespoon Herb Butter under skin. Rub turkey inside and out with remaining Herb Butter; sprinkle with salt and pepper. Place onion, celery and lemon inside turkey. Insert a meat thermometer into thickest part of thigh; cover loosely with aluminum foil. Roast at 325 degrees for 2-1/2 hours; remove aluminum foil to allow browning. Roast for an additional hour, basting with drippings every 20 minutes, until thermometer reads 180 degrees. Transfer turkey to platter, reserving drippings for gravy. Re-cover with aluminum foil; let rest for 15 to 20 minutes before carving. Serves 12 to 14.

Herb Butter:

1 lb. butter, softened
4 t. lemon juice
1/2 t. garlic powder
1 t. dried oregano
1 t. dried chives
1 t. dried thyme
1 t. dried rosemary
1 t. dried tarragon

Blend butter, lemon juice and garlic powder. Crush herbs finely; stir into butter mixture. Form into a log; wrap tightly with plastic wrap and chill overnight. Makes 2 cups.

Turkey Gravy:

Pour pan juices into a bowl; let stand 10 minutes. Skim off fat; measure out 6 tablespoons, discarding remaining fat. Measure skimmed pan juices. Add turkey broth to measure 3 cups; set aside. Cook fat in a skillet over low heat until bubbly. Gradually whisk in 6 tablespoons quick-mixing or all-purpose flour until smooth and bubbly. Slowly stir in reserved pan juices; heat to boiling, stirring constantly until thickened. Add salt and pepper to taste. Makes 3 cups.

Thanks

Cranberry-Apple Glazed Turkey

This version of our roast turkey combines a great blend of flavors.

Prepare turkey as directed on preceding page, using 6 tablespoons plain butter instead of Herb Butter and an apple instead of the lemon. Roast as directed. About 20 minutes before turkey is done, brush with Cranberry-Apple Glaze. Brush with any remaining glaze before carving.

Cranberry-Apple Glaze:

8-oz. can jellied cranberry sauce
1/4 c. apple jelly
1/4 c. light corn syrup

Combine ingredients in a small saucepan over medium heat for about 5 minutes, stirring occasionally, until melted and smooth.

Nutty Sausage & Cranberry Stuffing

A savory and sweet classic stuffing.

16-oz. pkg. cornbread stuffing mix
2 c. chicken broth
1 egg, beaten
1/2 c. butter, divided
1 c. onion, chopped
1 c. celery, chopped
1 c. ground Italian pork sausage, browned and drained
1 c. sweetened, dried cranberries
1/2 c. chopped pecans

Prepare stuffing mix according to package directions, using broth, egg and 1/4 cup butter; set aside. Sauté onion and celery in remaining butter until translucent. Stir onion mixture and remaining ingredients into stuffing; toss well to coat. Spread in a lightly greased 13"x9" baking pan. Cover and bake at 350 degrees for 30 minutes. Serves 8 to 10.

A fall delight that's oh-so easy to make...a gourmet chocolate apple. Simply insert a wooden stick into an apple, then coat the apple in melted caramel; set on wax paper to cool. When the caramel is firm, drizzle apple with melted chocolate and sprinkle with chopped nuts.

29

Garlicky Parmesan Asparagus

The garlic adds extra flavor.

1 T. butter
1/4 c. olive oil
2 cloves garlic, minced
1 lb. asparagus spears, trimmed
2 t. lemon juice
salt and pepper to taste
2 T. grated Parmesan cheese

Combine butter and olive oil in a skillet over medium heat. Add garlic; sauté for one to 2 minutes. Add asparagus and cook to desired tenderness, stirring occasionally, about 10 minutes. Drain asparagus; sprinkle with lemon juice, salt and pepper. Arrange on serving platter and sprinkle with Parmesan. Makes 4 servings.

Farmhouse Apple Bread

A mouthwatering treat during apple season.

3 eggs, beaten
2 c. sugar
1 c. oil
1 T. vanilla extract
3 c. all-purpose flour
1 t. baking soda
1 t. cinnamon
3 to 4 apples, cored, peeled and
  chopped
1 c. chopped pecans

Combine eggs, sugar, oil and vanilla until well mixed; set aside. Combine flour, baking soda and cinnamon in a separate bowl; stir into egg mixture. Fold in apples and pecans. Divide equally between 2 greased and floured 9"x5" loaf pans. Bake at 325 degrees for one hour and 10 minutes. Makes 2 loaves.

Mom's Apple-Cranberry Pie

Marbled Pumpkin Cheesecake

This cheesecake is a scrumptious ending to your Thanksgiving dinner.

3/4 c. gingersnaps, crushed
3/4 c. graham crackers, crushed
1/4 c. butter, melted
1-1/4 c. sugar, divided
2 8-oz. pkgs. cream cheese, softened
4 eggs
15-oz. can pumpkin
1/2 t. cinnamon
1/4 t. ground ginger
1/4 t. nutmeg
Optional: caramel ice cream topping

Combine gingersnaps, graham crackers, butter and 1/4 cup sugar in a medium bowl. Press into the bottom of an ungreased 9" round springform pan. Bake at 350 degrees for 8 to 10 minutes; cool. Beat cream cheese in a large bowl until smooth. Gradually add remaining sugar; beat until light. Add eggs one at a time, beating well after each. Transfer 1-1/2 cups of cream cheese mixture to a separate bowl; blend in pumpkin and spices. Pour half of pumpkin mixture into prepared crust; top with half of cream cheese mixture. Repeat layers. Using a table knife, cut through layers with an uplifting motion in 4 to 5 places to create marbled effect. Bake at 325 degrees for 45 minutes without opening oven door; turn off oven and let cheesecake stand in oven for one hour. Remove from oven; run knife around sides of pan to remove pan. Cool; keep refrigerated. If desired, drizzle with caramel topping. Makes 8 to 10 servings.

Tangy Turkey Cobb Salad   *Marbled Pumpkin Cheesecake*

Crustless Pumpkin Pie

Deliciously different!

4 eggs, beaten
15-oz. can pumpkin
12-oz. can evaporated milk
1-1/2 c. sugar
2 t. pumpkin pie spice
1 t. salt
18-1/2 oz. pkg. yellow cake mix
1 c. chopped pecans
1 c. butter, melted
Optional: whipped topping, chopped
    walnuts, cinnamon or nutmeg

Combine eggs, pumpkin, evaporated
milk, sugar, spice and salt. Mix well and
pour into an ungreased 13"x9" baking
pan. Sprinkle cake mix and nuts over
top. Drizzle with butter; do not stir.
Bake at 350 degrees for 45 minutes to
one hour, testing for doneness with a
toothpick. Serve with whipped topping
sprinkled with nuts and cinnamon or
nutmeg, if desired. Makes 8 to
10 servings.

Crustless Pumpkin Pie

Mom's Apple-Cranberry Pie

The fragrant aroma of fall will fill the air while this delicious pie is baking.

1 c. sugar, divided
1 t. cinnamon, divided
1/3 c. water
2 T. all-purpose flour
1 t. orange zest
4 Golden Delicious apples, cored,
    peeled and sliced
1-1/2 c. cranberries
2 9-inch pie crusts
1 egg white, beaten
Optional: vanilla ice cream

Combine one teaspoon sugar and 1/8 teaspoon cinnamon; set aside. Combine remaining sugar and cinnamon, water, flour and zest in a large saucepan; stir in apples and cranberries. Bring to a boil. Reduce heat and simmer for 10 to 15 minutes or until cranberries burst, stirring occasionally. Remove from heat; cool. Arrange one crust in a 9" pie plate. Spoon apple mixture into crust; top with remaining crust. Trim and flute edges; cut vents in crust. Brush crust with egg white; sprinkle with reserved sugar-cinnamon mixture. Cover edges of crust with aluminum foil. Bake at 375 degrees for 25 minutes; remove foil and bake an additional 20 to 25 minutes, until crust is golden and filling is bubbly. Serve warm, with scoops of ice cream if desired. Serves 6 to 8.

Top slices of warm pie with homemade whipped cream. In a chilled bowl, use an electric mixer to blend 2 cups heavy whipping cream, then gradually add 1/4 cup sugar and beat until stiff. Make it even more special by adding 2 drops of pumpkin or hazelnut flavoring, or a dash of espresso powder.

Tangy Turkey Cobb Salad

Leftover turkey is sliced and served alongside salad favorites, then drizzled with an out-of-this-world cranberry vinaigrette.

6-oz. pkg. baby lettuce or spinach
2 c. roast turkey breast, sliced into strips
6 slices bacon, crisply cooked and
    crumbled
15-oz. can mandarin oranges, drained
1/2 lb. asparagus spears, trimmed and
    steamed
1 avocado, pitted and sliced
1/2 c. red onion, thinly sliced
4-oz. container crumbled blue cheese
3/4 c. toasted pecans, coarsely chopped
1 c. sliced mushrooms

Place lettuce or spinach on a large serving platter. Arrange remaining ingredients in sections across platter. Drizzle with Cranberry Vinaigrette or pass dressing separately. Makes 4 to 6 servings.

Cranberry Vinaigrette:

1 c. jellied cranberry sauce
5 T. red wine vinegar
4 T. olive oil
1 T. sugar

Break up cranberry sauce with a fork. Whisk in vinegar until blended; slowly stir in oil and sugar until sugar dissolves. Keep refrigerated.

Golden Shepherd's Pie

The day after Thanksgiving, you'll appreciate this quick-to-fix comfort food.

2 to 3 c. prepared stuffing
1 c. cooked green beans, broccoli,
    carrots or other vegetables
2-1/2 c. roast turkey, cubed or sliced
1 to 2 c. turkey gravy
2 c. mashed potatoes
1/4 c. butter, diced
Garnish: shredded Cheddar cheese,
    paprika, parsley

In a lightly greased 10" deep-dish pie plate or 4 oven-safe bowls, layer stuffing, vegetables, turkey and gravy. Spread or pipe mashed potatoes over top; dot with butter and sprinkle with garnishes as desired. Bake at 350 degrees for 25 to 35 minutes, until heated through and golden. Serves 4.

Thanks

Hearty Turkey Vegetable Soup

A soup to warm you on a crisp autumn day.

2 T. oil
1/2 c. onion, diced
2 cloves garlic, minced
8 c. turkey or chicken broth
3 c. roast turkey, diced
1/2 c. carrots, peeled and diced
1/2 c. celery, diced
1 to 2 potatoes, peeled and diced
1/2 c. quick-cooking barley, uncooked
2 c. cooked green beans, corn, broccoli
    or other vegetables, chopped
1 T. dried parsley
1 t. dried marjoram
salt and pepper to taste

Heat oil in a large heavy stockpot over medium heat. Add onion and garlic; sauté for 3 to 4 minutes. Add broth and bring to a boil; reduce heat. Add remaining ingredients; cover and simmer gently for 35 to 40 minutes, until potatoes and barley are tender. Makes 6 to 8 servings.

Homemade Turkey Broth:

1 roast turkey carcass
12 c. water
2 carrots, coarsely chopped
2 stalks celery, coarsely chopped
2 onions, coarsely chopped
1 t. whole peppercorns
6 sprigs fresh parsley
6 sprigs fresh thyme
1 bay leaf

Slice any meat from carcass; refrigerate for soup or other use. Place carcass in a large heavy stockpot, breaking to fit as necessary. Add remaining ingredients. Bring to a boil; reduce heat to low and simmer for 2 to 3 hours, skimming any foam from the surface. Strain and cool broth, discarding vegetables and herbs. Refrigerate broth; skim fat from surface before using. Makes about 10 cups.

Add zip to leftover mashed potatoes...it's easy! Stir in sour cream, shredded cheese, cream cheese or crisply crumbled bacon to taste. Spoon mixture into a baking dish, dot with butter and heat through in the oven or microwave.

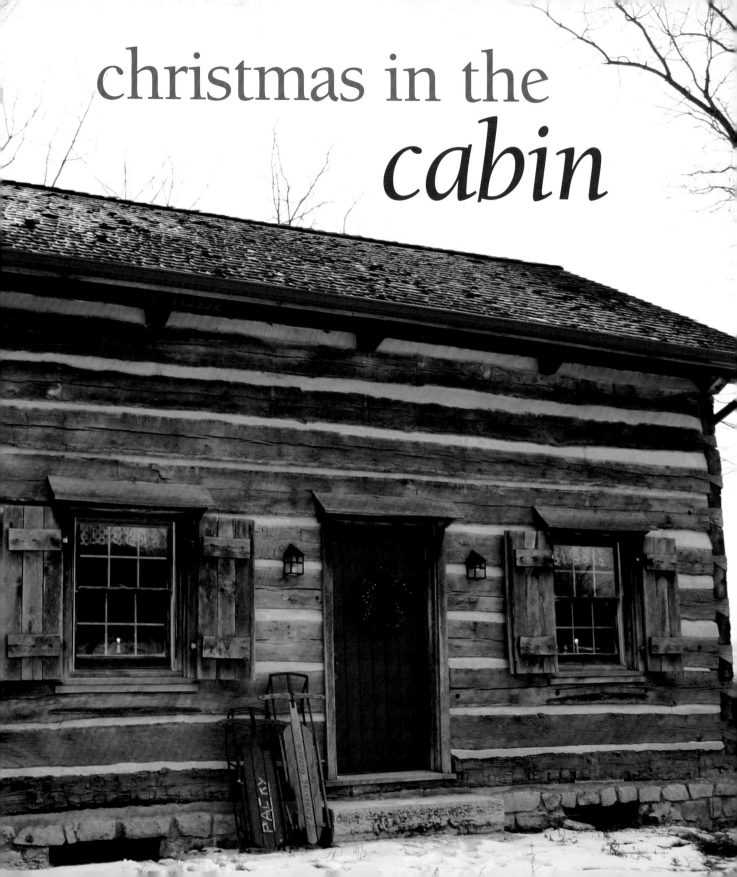

christmas in the
cabin

Nutty Maple Waffles

Red & Green Jewels

A candle flickers at each window, wreaths of bay leaves and berries hang on every door, and the air is filled with the fresh scent of balsam...welcome to Christmas in the cabin. Brush the snow from your boots, open the door and you'll be greeted with the joys of the season. The tree is up, a fire crackles in the fireplace and out come the warm woolens and homespun blankets.

No matter where we are, traditional holiday foods have a special place all their own. On Christmas Eve the mingling aromas of Pineapple-Honey Glazed Ham, Rosemary & Garlic Potatoes and Herbed Cheddar Biscuits fill us with anticipation of the meal to come. Sweet endings to dinner, slices of Old-Fashioned Gingerbread Torte and cups of Creamy Eggnog Punch, are sure to bring visions of sugarplums.

When Christmas finally arrives, Overnight Raisin French Toast and Nutty Maple Waffles are quick to prepare so the magic of the morning can linger on.

It's Christmas! Go sledding, build a snowman and roast marshmallows at the hearth...make it a day to remember.

PINEAPPLE-HONEY GLAZED HAM

HERBED CHEDDAR BISCUITS

ROSEMARY & GARLIC POTATOES

GRANDMA'S GELATIN SALAD

CREAMY EGGNOG PUNCH

FUDGY MINT BROWNIES

RED & GREEN JEWELS

DREAMY CHOCOLATE PECAN PIE

OLD-FASHIONED GINGERBREAD TORTE

FRIENDSHIP TEA

OVERNIGHT RAISIN FRENCH TOAST

NUTTY MAPLE WAFFLES

COUNTRY-STYLE SKILLET APPLES

CLASSIC QUICHE LORRAINE

LEMONY BLUEBERRY SCONE MIX

CHOCOLATE SWIRLED BANANA BREAD

Pineapple-Honey Glazed Ham
and Herbed Cheddar Biscuits

Rosemary &
Garlic Potatoes

Pineapple-Honey Glazed Ham

Topping the ham with a honey glaze keeps it moist and delicious.

10 to 14-lb. fully-cooked
    smoked spiral-sliced ham
6-oz. can frozen orange juice
    concentrate, thawed
1 c. honey
1/3 c. soy sauce
1/3 c. pineapple preserves
1/2 t. nutmeg
1/4 t. ground cloves

Place ham in a roasting pan; insert
meat thermometer into thickest
part of ham. For glaze, stir together
remaining ingredients in a medium
bowl; set aside. Bake ham at
325 degrees for 30 minutes;
remove from oven and pour glaze
over ham. Return to oven; bake for an
additional 30 minutes to one hour, until
ham is heated through and internal
temperature of 140 degrees is reached.
Makes 16 to 20 servings.

Herbed Cheddar Biscuits

*Serve with dinner, or for breakfast split
and topped with slices of warm ham.*

2-1/2 c. biscuit baking mix
1 c. shredded Cheddar cheese
3/4 c. milk
1/8 t. garlic powder
1/4 c. plus 2 T. butter, melted and
    divided
1/2 t. garlic salt
Optional: 1/2 t. dried parsley

Combine baking mix, cheese, milk,
garlic powder and 2 tablespoons butter;
mix well. Form mixture into balls by
1/4 cupfuls; arrange on an ungreased
baking sheet. Bake at 400 degrees for
14 to 16 minutes. Mix together
remaining butter, garlic salt and
parsley, if using; brush over biscuits
before serving. Makes one dozen.

Rosemary & Garlic Potatoes

*Simple to prepare so there's more time
for shaking packages!*

2 lbs. redskin potatoes, sliced
1/4 c. olive oil
1 T. dried rosemary, crumbled
garlic powder to taste
salt and pepper to taste

Combine all ingredients together in
a large bowl; toss to coat. Arrange
on an ungreased baking sheet. Bake
at 400 degrees for 25 to 35 minutes,
until tender. Serves 4 to 6.

*Traditionally, stockings are hung by the mantel
just waiting to be filled with sweet treats and
surprises. But this year, why not try something
new? Hang pairs of mittens or fleece hats and
snow caps instead of stockings. Sure to bring
giggles...set out playful rubber boots or cowboy
boots to be filled by Santa!*

Grandma's Gelatin Salad

No holiday dinner would be complete without this old-fashioned favorite.

6-oz. pkg. lime gelatin mix
1 c. boiling water
2 c. mini marshmallows
9-oz. can crushed pineapple
1/8 t. salt
8-oz. container small-curd cottage
   cheese
16-oz. container frozen whipped
   topping, thawed and divided
1/2 c. chopped pecans

In a medium bowl, dissolve gelatin mix in boiling water. Stir in marshmallows, pineapple and salt. Chill for 30 to 40 minutes, until thickened but not set. Add cottage cheese, one cup whipped topping and pecans; spoon into a 9"x9" glass serving dish. Chill until set. Cut into squares; top each square with a dollop of remaining whipped topping. Makes 9 servings.

Creamy Eggnog Punch

Set the punch bowl in the middle of a wreath topped with glittering stars.

2 qts. dairy eggnog
2 8-oz. containers French vanilla
   frozen whipped topping, thawed
   and divided
1 t. cinnamon
2 t. rum extract
1 c. ice cubes
Garnish: nutmeg

Whisk together eggnog, one container whipped topping and cinnamon in a large bowl until blended. Add extract and ice cubes; mix well. Chill. At serving time, top with dollops of remaining topping; sprinkle to taste with nutmeg. Makes 30 servings.

the cabin

Fudgy Mint Brownies

Mmmm...leave these out for Santa!

20-oz. pkg. brownie mix
1/2 c. whipping cream
1/2 c. cream cheese, softened
1/4 c. powdered sugar
1/2 t. peppermint extract
several drops red food coloring
Garnish: peppermint candies, crushed

Prepare brownie mix according to package directions. Bake in 18 to 24 paper-lined mini muffin cups. Let cool. In a medium bowl, beat cream with an electric mixer on high speed until soft peaks form. Set aside. In another bowl, beat together cream cheese, powdered sugar, extract and coloring on low speed until blended; increase to medium speed and beat until smooth. Gently fold in whipped cream. Spread over brownies; garnish with crushed candies. Makes 1-1/2 to 2 dozen.

Red & Green Jewels

Soft cookies filled with candied cherries and toasted pecans.

1 c. butter, softened
2/3 c. brown sugar, packed
1 egg
2 t. vanilla extract
1/2 t. salt
2 c. all-purpose flour
3/4 c. chopped pecans, toasted
1/2 c. candied red and green cherries, chopped

In a large bowl, soften butter with an electric mixer on low speed. Beat in brown sugar, egg, vanilla and salt. Beat in as much flour as possible; stir in any remaining flour by hand. Stir in pecans and cherries. Drop dough by rounded teaspoonfuls onto ungreased baking sheets, 2 inches apart. Bake at 375 degrees for 8 to 10 minutes, until lightly golden. Cool on a wire rack. Makes about 2-1/2 dozen.

This year celebrate St. Nicholas Day on December 6th. It's said when a pair of shoes is left by the fireplace the night before, you'll wake up to find them filled with sweets!

Dreamy Chocolate Pecan Pie

Chocolatey, crunchy and sweet...this pie is sure to please.

3 eggs
1 c. light corn syrup
1 c. sugar
2 T. margarine, melted
1 t. vanilla extract
1/8 t. salt
1 c. pecan halves
1/2 c. semi-sweet chocolate chips
9-inch pie crust

Beat eggs slightly in a medium bowl; blend in syrup, sugar, margarine, vanilla and salt. Stir in pecans and chocolate chips. Pour into pie crust. Bake at 400 degrees for 15 minutes; reduce oven to 350 degrees. Bake for an additional 25 to 30 minutes, until golden and puffed on top. Cool before serving. Serves 8.

A tabletop tree in the kitchen is sure to stir up memories. Decorate your tree with cookie cutters, mini kitchen gadgets, plump stuffed hearts or stars, vintage crocheted potholders and jolly gingerbread men cookies. A popcorn, cranberry or ribbon garland will give it a festive finishing touch. Now simply tuck your tree into a Mason jar, crock or even a tea towel-lined colander!

Dreamy Chocolate Pecan Pie

Old-Fashioned
Gingerbread Torte

Old-Fashioned Gingerbread Torte

You'll love this gingerbread cake with its rich, buttercream frosting.

3 c. all-purpose flour
3/4 t. baking soda
3/4 t. salt
1 T. ground ginger
1-1/2 t. cinnamon
1-1/2 c. light molasses
1 c. water
3/4 c. butter, softened
3/4 c. sugar
2 eggs

Stir together flour, baking soda, salt and spices in a medium bowl; set aside. Whisk together molasses and water in another medium bowl; set aside. In a large bowl, beat butter and sugar until blended with an electric mixer on low speed. Increase speed to high; beat until creamy, about 2 minutes. Reduce speed to low; add eggs, one at a time, beating well after each. Add flour mixture alternately with molasses mixture; beat until blended. Line bottoms of three, 8" round cake pans with wax paper; grease and flour pans. Spread batter in pans. Bake at 350 degrees for 25 to 30 minutes, until a toothpick tests clean.

Cool in pans on wire racks for 10 minutes; turn cakes out onto racks and cool completely. Discard wax paper. Assemble cake with Buttercream Frosting; chill until serving time. Makes 16 servings.

Buttercream Frosting:

1 c. butter, softened
6 to 7 c. powdered sugar
6 to 9 T. milk
2 t. vanilla extract
1/4 t. salt
1/2 c. white chocolate chips, melted
     and cooled

Beat butter until very fluffy. Add sugar and milk in small batches, beating after each addition until very fluffy. Stir in vanilla, salt and melted chocolate. Use immediately.

Chocolate curls dress up any dessert and are so easy to make. Simply use a vegetable peeler with a long narrow blade and a bar of room-temperature chocolate. Be sure your peeler is absolutely dry. Make curls by pressing down the peeler along the smoothest, widest side of the chocolate bar. The harder you press, the thicker the curls will be. Refrigerate curls until ready to use.

Friendship Tea

A steaming mug of this tea is sure to take the chill off on a frosty winter night.

6 c. water, divided
3 teabags
1 c. sugar
1 stick cinnamon
1 t. whole cloves
12-oz. can pineapple juice
1 c. orange juice
lemon juice to taste

Bring 2 cups water to a boil in a small saucepan. Remove from heat; add teabags and let stand for 5 minutes. In a medium saucepan, combine remaining water, sugar, cinnamon and cloves; bring to a boil and simmer for 10 minutes. Discard teabags; add brewed tea to sugar mixture. Stir; add juices and simmer until heated through. Strain before serving. Serves 6 to 8.

Overnight Raisin French Toast

This French toast, baked in the oven, melts in your mouth.

1 c. light corn syrup
1 c. brown sugar, packed
1 c. butter
12 slices raisin bread
6 eggs
2 c. milk
1 t. vanilla extract

In a saucepan over medium heat, bring corn syrup, brown sugar and butter to a boil. Boil for 5 minutes; pour into a greased 13"x9" baking pan. Arrange half the bread slices in the pan; top with remaining bread slices and set aside. Beat together eggs, milk and vanilla; pour over bread. Cover with aluminum foil and refrigerate overnight. Uncover; bake at 350 degrees for 45 minutes. Serve slices with warm glaze from pan as syrup. Makes 6 to 8 servings.

Nutty Maple Waffles

Crunchy pecans paired with maple...a great way to begin the day.

1-1/2 c. all-purpose flour
2 T. sugar
1 t. baking powder
1/4 t. salt
2 eggs, separated
12-oz. can evaporated milk
3 T. oil
1/2 t. maple extract
1/2 c. pecans, finely chopped

Combine flour, sugar, baking powder and salt in a medium bowl; mix well and set aside. Combine egg yolks, evaporated milk, oil and extract in a large bowl; blend well. Gradually add flour mixture, beating well after each addition; set aside. In a small bowl, beat egg whites with an electric mixer on high until stiff peaks form; fold into batter. For each waffle, pour 1/2 cup batter onto preheated, greased waffle iron; sprinkle with one tablespoon nuts. Bake according to manufacturer's instructions. Makes 8 waffles.

Country-Style Skillet Apples

Try tart Granny Smith or Jonathan apples in this recipe...both are terrific choices.

1/3 c. butter
1/2 c. sugar
1/2 t. cinnamon
2 T. cornstarch
1 c. water
4 cooking apples, cored, peeled
   and sliced

Melt butter in a skillet over medium heat. Stir in sugar, cinnamon and cornstarch; mix well and stir in water. Add apples. Cook over medium heat, stirring occasionally, until tender, about 10 minutes. Makes 4 to 6 servings.

Some Christmas cards are just too sweet to tuck away...so display them! Hung from ribbons across a mantel or window, or arranged on a vintage-style wire card holder, they're a constant reminder of family & friends. Add some favorite photos or even handmade gift tags and you've easily created a sentimental remembrance to enjoy year after year.

Classic Quiche Lorraine

A tried & true recipe that's perfect for either breakfast or dinner.

9-inch pie crust
8 slices bacon, crisply cooked and
    crumbled, drippings reserved
1 onion, chopped
3 eggs
1-1/2 c. half-and-half
1/4 t. salt
1/4 t. pepper
1/8 t. nutmeg
1-1/2 c. shredded Swiss or
    Gruyère cheese

Arrange pie crust in a 9-inch pie plate; press a double layer of aluminum foil into crust. Bake at 450 degrees for 8 minutes; remove aluminum foil and bake an additional 4 to 5 minutes, until crust is set. Cool on a wire rack. Sauté onion in one tablespoon reserved drippings until tender; drain. Spoon bacon and onion evenly into baked crust. In a large bowl, whisk together eggs, half-and-half and seasonings; add cheese and whisk to combine. Pour into crust; set pie plate on a baking sheet. Bake at 450 degrees for 35 to 40 minutes until quiche is golden, puffed and a knife inserted in center comes out clean. If necessary, cover edges of crust with foil to prevent burning. Remove from oven; let stand 15 minutes before serving. Makes 6 servings.

Overnight Raisin French Toast

Lemony Blueberry Scone Mix

This easy mix makes delicious scones in no time at all.

2 c. all-purpose flour
1/3 c. sugar
1/4 c. powdered milk or powdered
    non-dairy creamer
2 t. baking powder
1 t. lemon zest
1/4 t. salt
1/3 c. shortening
1 c. dried blueberries

In a large bowl, mix together flour, sugar, powdered milk or creamer, baking powder, zest and salt. Cut in shortening with a pastry blender until mixture resembles coarse crumbs; stir in berries. Place mixture in a one-quart plastic zipping bag. Seal tightly; attach instructions.

Instructions:

Whisk together one egg and 1/4 cup water in a large bowl. Add scone mix; stir just until moistened. Turn dough out onto a lightly floured surface; knead for 12 to 15 strokes, until smooth. Pat into an 8-inch circle. Cut into 10 wedges; place wedges one inch apart on an ungreased baking sheet. Brush tops with milk; sprinkle with sugar. Bake at 400 degrees for 12 to 15 minutes, until golden. Serve warm. Makes 10 scones.

Country-Style Skillet Apples

Classic Quiche Lorraine

Blueberry
Scone Mix

Lemony Blueberry
Scone Mix

Chocolate Swirled
Banana Bread

Chocolate Swirled Banana Bread

Our favorite quick bread gets a chocolate twist.

3/4 c. plus 2 T. butter, softened
   and divided
1/3 c. finely chopped walnuts
1-1/4 c. plus 2 T. sugar, divided
2 c. all-purpose flour
2 t. baking powder
1/4 t. baking soda
1/4 t. salt
3 ripe bananas, mashed
2 t. vanilla extract
3 eggs
6 T. buttermilk
4 1-oz. sqs. semi-sweet baking
   chocolate, melted and cooled

Generously spread two, 8"x4" loaf pans with 2 tablespoons butter. Mix walnuts and 2 tablespoons sugar; press into buttered pans and set aside. Combine flour, baking powder, baking soda and salt; mix well and set aside. Combine remaining butter, remaining sugar, bananas and vanilla in a separate bowl. Beat with an electric mixer on medium speed until well blended. Beat in eggs, one at a time, just until mixed. Add half of flour mixture, all the buttermilk and remaining flour mixture, stirring well after each addition. Spoon half the batter into a separate bowl; gently stir in melted chocolate. Add both batters by large spoonfuls, alternately, to prepared pans. Gently run a knife tip through batter to swirl. Bake at 350 degrees for about 35 minutes, until a toothpick comes out nearly clean. Cool in pan on a wire rack for 15 minutes. Gently tap sides of pans on counter to loosen. Invert onto rack; cool completely. Makes 2 loaves.

Choose a winter's afternoon and spend the day baking a yummy gingerbread house. Purchase a kit to keep construction time to a minimum, then get right to the fun of decorating. A row of gumdrops makes a sparkly fence, candy canes become trees and peppermint candies make a magical walkway. Top off your house with a dusting of powdered sugar as freshly fallen snow.

Sunday *dinner*

*Grandma's
Dinner Rolls*

Sweet Ambrosia Salad

A sapphire-blue sky and the heavenly scent of lilac blossoms fills the air...it's spring in the country. There's no better time for leisurely Sunday dinners than during warm, breezy afternoons we wish would never end. Dinner at Grandma's is a simple country pleasure we never tire of looking forward to...the swaying of a porch swing, the familiar creaking of the screen door and the tantalizing aromas that fill the house.

Dinner is hearty, old-fashioned and served country-style. Pork Chops with Herbed Stuffing, Buttery Scalloped Potatoes, Brown Sugar-Glazed Carrots and Grandma's Dinner Rolls are passed around the table. Dandy Deviled Eggs and Sweet Ambrosia Salad are favorites we can count on and somehow we can always find room for a slice of Pineapple Upside-Down Cake!

Sunday dinners are a happy time...children laughing, sweet remembrances and memories being made. Afterwards, take a drive down a long country road and enjoy the soft light of a late afternoon in spring.

OVERNIGHT LAYERED SALAD

COUNTRY-STYLE 3-BEAN SALAD

SWEET AMBROSIA SALAD

BUTTERY SCALLOPED POTATOES

BROWN SUGAR-GLAZED CARROTS

PORK CHOPS WITH HERBED STUFFING

OLD-FASHIONED APPLESAUCE

DANDY DEVILED EGGS

GRANDMA'S DINNER ROLLS

STRAWBERRY-RHUBARB FREEZER JAM

PINEAPPLE UPSIDE-DOWN CAKE

MILE-HIGH CHOCOLATE MERINGUE PIE

Country-Style 3-Bean Salad

*Pretty posies make
for an old-fashioned
welcome on a front door.
Large blooms like
peonies or lilacs
can be tucked into
water-filled vintage-style
bottles, then wrapped
in wide ribbon and
secured to a
wreath hanger.*

Overnight Layered Salad

*Add any favorites to this recipe...shredded
carrots, sweetened, dried cranberries or
mandarin oranges. The layering is so
pretty; a glass bowl is a must!*

1 head lettuce, torn into bite-size
    pieces
1 to 2 red onions, thinly sliced and
    separated into rings
10-oz. pkg. frozen peas
3 to 4 eggs, hard-boiled, peeled
    and sliced
4 radishes, thinly sliced
1/4 lb. bacon, crisply cooked
    and crumbled
8-oz. jar mayonnaise
1-1/2 c. grated Parmesan cheese

Arrange lettuce in a large bowl.
Top with onions, frozen peas, eggs,
radishes and bacon. Spoon mayonnaise
completely over top; sprinkle with
Parmesan. Cover and refrigerate
overnight. Makes 8 to 10 servings.

Overnight Layered Salad

Country-Style 3-Bean Salad

*A traditional recipe that's a must-have for
any family gathering.*

14-1/2 oz. can green beans, drained
14-1/2 oz. can yellow wax beans,
   drained
15-1/2 oz. can kidney beans, drained
   and rinsed
1 red onion, thinly sliced
3/4 c. sugar
2/3 c. vinegar
1/3 c. oil
1 t. salt
1/4 t. pepper
1/4 t. dried oregano

Toss beans and onion together in
a large bowl; set aside. Combine
remaining ingredients in a small
saucepan over medium heat. Cook
and stir until sugar dissolves; pour
over bean mixture. Cover and chill
overnight. Makes 10 to 12 servings.

Sweet Ambrosia Salad

It wouldn't be Grandma's without this!

20-oz. can pineapple chunks, drained
14-1/2 oz. jar maraschino cherries,
   drained
11-oz. can mandarin oranges, drained
8-oz. container sour cream
10-1/2 oz. pkg. pastel mini
   marshmallows
1/2 c. sweetened flaked coconut

Combine fruit in a large bowl; stir
in sour cream until coated. Fold in
marshmallows and coconut; cover and
chill overnight. Makes 8 to 10 servings.

dinner

Buttery Scalloped Potatoes

*Tender, creamy potatoes...an
all-time favorite.*

2 T. all-purpose flour
1 t. salt
1/4 t. pepper
4 c. potatoes, peeled and thinly sliced
2/3 c. sweet onion, thinly sliced
2 T. butter, sliced
1-1/2 c. milk
Garnish: paprika

Mix together flour, salt and pepper;
set aside. In a greased 2-quart casserole
dish, layer half each of potatoes, onion,
flour mixture and butter. Repeat
layering with remaining potatoes,
onion, flour mixture and butter. Set
aside. Heat milk just to boiling and
pour over top; sprinkle with paprika.
Bake, covered, at 375 degrees for
45 minutes. Uncover and bake an
additional 10 minutes. Serves 8.

Brown Sugar-Glazed Carrots

*Exceptionally good and so simple
to prepare!*

1 lb. carrots, peeled and halved
   lengthwise
1/2 c. orange juice
5 T. brown sugar, packed
2 T. butter
1/8 t. salt

Cover carrots with water in a medium
saucepan. Boil until tender; drain and
return to saucepan. Add orange juice
and simmer over low heat until juice
is nearly evaporated. Stir in remaining
ingredients; continue cooking until
butter is melted and carrots are glazed.
Makes 4 to 6 servings.

*Vintage-look storage jars show off sentimental
treasures too pretty to store away. Filled with
buttons or baubles, favorite photos, postcards
or a mix of sun-washed seashells, they add
a sweet touch of nostalgia to any room.*

Pork Chops with Herbed Stuffing

Fresh herbs and garlic make for a very savory stuffing.

1 T. butter
1/4 c. olive oil, divided
1/2 c. onion, finely chopped
3/4 c. celery, finely chopped
1 c. cubed herb-seasoned stuffing
1/2 c. plus 3 T. chicken broth, divided
2 T. fresh parsley, minced
1 T. fresh thyme, minced
salt and pepper to taste
4 thick bone-in pork chops, sliced
    horizontally to the bone
2 cloves garlic, minced
1/2 t. salt
1/4 c. dry sherry or chicken broth

Heat butter and one tablespoon oil in an oven-proof skillet over medium heat. Sauté onion and celery until soft, about 3 minutes. Transfer mixture to a medium bowl; add stuffing, 3 tablespoons broth, herbs, salt and pepper and toss well. Spoon stuffing equally into pork chops; set aside. Place garlic, one tablespoon oil and salt in a cup; mix with a fork and rub over chops. Heat remaining oil in same skillet; cook chops until golden on both sides. Transfer skillet to oven; bake at 350 degrees until done, about 15 minutes. Arrange chops on a serving plate; keep warm. For gravy, add remaining broth and sherry or broth to skillet; cook and stir over medium-high heat until reduced by half. Serve gravy with pork chops. Makes 4 servings.

Buttery Scalloped Potatoes

Old-Fashioned Applesauce

For the best flavor, use a tart apple such as Granny Smith, Cortland or Rome Beauty.

2 lbs. apples, cored, peeled and cubed
1 c. water
1 T. lemon juice
1/4 to 1/2 c. sugar
1/2 t. cinnamon

Combine apples, water and lemon juice in a large saucepan; bring to a boil over high heat. Reduce heat; cover and simmer until apples are tender, 10 to 15 minutes. Uncover and cook until thickened, stirring frequently, about 10 minutes. Stir in sugar to taste and cinnamon; cover and chill overnight. Makes 6 to 8 servings.

Dandy Deviled Eggs

Instead of slicing the eggs horizontally, try this! Oh-so pretty when served in old-fashioned egg cups.

6 eggs, hard-boiled and peeled
1/4 c. mayonnaise
1-1/2 T. sweet pickle relish
1 t. mustard
salt and pepper to taste
Garnish: paprika

Slice off top one-third of eggs; make a thin slice from bottom so eggs will sit upright. With a small spoon, scoop out yolks and place in a small bowl. Mash yolks with a fork; stir in mayonnaise, relish, mustard, salt and pepper. Spoon yolk mixture into eggs; sprinkle with paprika. Makes 6 servings.

Pineapple Upside-Down Cake

Grandma's Dinner Rolls

Crescent-shaped and flaky...irresistible topped with butter.

1 env. active dry yeast
1/2 c. plus 1 T. sugar, divided
3 eggs
1 c. warm water (110 to 115 degrees)
1/2 c. butter-flavored shortening
3/4 c. salt
5-1/4 to 5-3/4 c. all-purpose flour,
　　divided
Optional: 1 egg white, 1 T. water,
　　sesame seed

Combine yeast and one tablespoon sugar in a large bowl; beat in eggs and warm water with a fork. Let stand for 15 minutes. With an electric mixer on low speed, beat in remaining sugar, shortening and salt. Add 2 cups flour and beat just until combined; beat on high speed for 3 minutes. With a spoon, stir in as much of remaining flour as possible. Turn out onto a lightly floured surface; add any remaining flour and knead for 6 to 8 minutes, until dough is smooth and elastic. Form into a ball; place in a greased bowl and turn to coat.

Cover and let rise in a warm place until double, one to 1-1/2 hours; or refrigerate for 8 hours to overnight. Punch down dough; divide into 2 balls and let stand for 10 minutes (20 minutes if dough was chilled). On a floured surface, roll out each ball to a 12-inch circle; slice each into 12 wedges. Starting at wide end, roll up each wedge crescent-style. Place rolls point-side down on a greased baking sheet. Cover and let rise in a warm place until nearly double, 30 to 45 minutes. If desired, whisk together egg white and water; brush over rolls and sprinkle with sesame seed. Bake at 375 degrees for 10 to 12 minutes, until golden. Serve warm. Makes 2 dozen.

dinner

Strawberry-Rhubarb Freezer Jam

This can remain frozen for up to a year...but it won't last that long!

1-1/4 c. strawberries, hulled and
    crushed
1/2 c. rhubarb, finely chopped
4 c. sugar
1 pouch liquid fruit pectin
1 T. lemon juice
5 1/2-pt. freezer-safe plastic
    containers, sterilized

Combine strawberries and rhubarb in a large bowl; stir in sugar. Let stand 10 minutes, stirring occasionally. In a small bowl, mix pectin and lemon juice. Add to fruit mixture and stir for 3 minutes, or until sugar is dissolved. Spoon into containers, leaving 1/2-inch headspace; secure lids. Let stand at room temperature for 24 hours before freezing. Thaw in refrigerator before using; keep refrigerated for up to 3 weeks. Makes 5 containers.

Herbs are happy growing in a sunny windowsill. Tuck them into Grandma's teacups or cream pitchers for a fresh look...a clever way to keep them right at your fingertips while cooking!

*Mile-High Chocolate
Meringue Pie*

Pineapple Upside-Down Cake

*Keep a pitcher of icy milk on hand...a perfect
pairing with this handed-down recipe.*

1/3 c. butter
1/2 c. brown sugar, packed
20-oz. can pineapple rings, drained and
    6 T. juice reserved
8 to 10 maraschino cherries
15 to 20 pecan halves
2 eggs
2/3 c. sugar
1 t. vanilla extract
1 c. all-purpose flour
1 t. baking powder
1/4 t. salt

Melt butter over low heat in a
10" cast iron skillet; sprinkle brown
sugar evenly over butter. Arrange
pineapple rings in skillet. Place a
cherry in the center of each ring;
arrange pecan halves around rings and
set aside. With an electric mixer on
high speed, beat eggs in a medium
bowl until thick and lemon-colored,
about 5 minutes. Gradually beat in
sugar; stir in reserved pineapple juice
and vanilla. Add flour, baking powder
and salt; mix well. Pour batter over
pineapple rings in skillet. Bake at
350 degrees for 30 to 35 minutes. Let
cool in skillet for 30 minutes. Invert
skillet on a serving plate; let stand
for a minute, then turn out of skillet.
Makes 10 to 12 servings.

Mile-High Chocolate Meringue Pie

With two yummy variations to this recipe, it will be hard to choose just one!

1-1/2 c. sugar
1/2 c. baking cocoa
1/4 t. salt
1/2 c. all-purpose flour
4 egg yolks, beaten
2 c. whole milk
1 t. vanilla extract
9-inch pie crust, baked and cooled

Mix sugar, cocoa, salt and flour in a medium bowl; set aside. Place egg yolks in a medium heavy saucepan; whisk in sugar mixture and milk alternately until smooth. Bring to a boil over medium heat; stir in vanilla. Boil, stirring constantly, until thickened, about 10 to 15 minutes. Remove from heat and beat until smooth; pour into crust. Spoon meringue over hot filling, sealing carefully to edge of crust. Bake at 350 degrees until meringue is lightly golden, 12 to 15 minutes. Cool completely. Serves 8.

Meringue:

5 to 6 egg whites
1/4 t. cream of tartar
6 T. sugar
1/2 t. vanilla extract

In a deep bowl, beat egg whites with an electric mixer on high speed until soft peaks form. Reduce mixer to low speed; add cream of tartar. Gradually beat in sugar, one tablespoon at a time; beat until stiff, glossy peaks form. Beat in vanilla.

Variation:

Coconut Cream Meringue Pie

1 c. sweetened flaked coconut
9-inch pie crust, baked and cooled
1 c. sugar
1/4 c. cornstarch
3 egg yolks, beaten
2-1/4 c. whole milk
1 t. vanilla extract

Sprinkle coconut in crust; set aside. Stir together sugar and cornstarch. Place egg yolks in a medium heavy saucepan; whisk in sugar mixture and milk alternately until smooth. Cook and stir over medium-high heat until boiling and thickened, about 10 to 15 minutes. Remove from heat and stir in vanilla; pour over coconut in crust. Spoon meringue over hot filling, sealing carefully to edge of crust. Bake at 325 degrees until meringue is lightly golden, 15 to 20 minutes. Serves 8.

When setting a table, the sweetest, simple touch can make a difference. A rolled and ribbon-tied linen napkin needs only tiny buttercup or violet blossoms tucked under the ribbon to make it extra-special.

bake *sale*

Candy Cones

*Luscious Lemon Layer Cake and
Celebration Cupcake Cones*

Streusel-Topped
Raspberry Bars

Sweet confections...chocolatey

cookies, fruit-filled bars, scrumptious cupcakes. Where can you find all these homemade delights? At an old-fashioned bake sale!

No matter if it's held during a hometown ball game or a grassy spot on the town square, bake sales are irresistible to everyone. And whether it's a local church or group of school moms, we know we'll be treated to bakers bringing out their very best for a good cause.

We've shared our favorite recipes for you to choose from. Big and little kids will love Celebration Cupcake Cones...a cupcake baked in an ice cream cone. Our Rocky Road Bars are filled to the brim with peanuts, marshmallows and chocolate chips, while Lemony Pecan Bars have a tangy taste that makes them disappear quickly from any bake sale table. Strawberry Delight Cookies are incredibly easy to make...they start with a cake mix. Top off these sweet treats with tall glasses of icy, Fresh-Squeezed Lemonade...refreshing and oh-so easy to prepare.

So have fun! You'll find having your own bake sale is one of the best ways to bring together family, friends and neighbors.

CELEBRATION CUPCAKE CONES

HOKEY-POKEY CUPCAKES

FRESH-SQUEEZED LEMONADE

TRIPLE-DELIGHT GERMAN CHOCOLATE CAKE

LUSCIOUS LEMON LAYER CAKE

CHOCOLATEY RICE POPS

SWEET SUCCESS TRAIL MIX

ROCKY ROAD BARS

6-LAYER BARS

LEMONY PECAN BARS

STREUSEL-TOPPED RASPBERRY BARS

PEANUT BUTTER BITES

STRAWBERRY DELIGHT COOKIES

BIG CHOCOLATE CHIP COOKIES

BEST-EVER BANANA BREAD

Celebration Cupcake Cones

*Use mini candy bars or chocolate drops
in these oh-so fun treats!*

18-1/4 oz. pkg. white or chocolate
    cake mix
24 flat-bottomed ice cream cones
24 mini candy bars, unwrapped
Garnish: candy sprinkles, maraschino
    cherries

Prepare cake mix according to package
directions. Spoon 1/8 cup batter into
each ice cream cone; push a candy bar
down all the way into batter in each
cone. Stand cones in muffin pans. Bake
at 350 degrees for 20 to 22 minutes,
or until a toothpick tests clean. Place
Swirl Frosting in a pastry bag with a
star tip; swirl frosting onto cones,
soft-serve ice cream style. Garnish as
desired. Makes 2 dozen cupcakes.

Swirl Frosting:

2 t. all-purpose flour
1/2 c. milk
1/4 c. shortening
1/4 c. butter
1/2 c. sugar
1/8 t. salt
1 t. vanilla extract
Optional: 1/4 t. almond extract

Mix flour and milk in a medium
saucepan over low heat. Cook and stir
until very thick and paste-like; let cool.
In a mixing bowl, blend shortening and
butter; add sugar and beat with an
electric mixer on high speed until fluffy.
Add flour mixture; continue beating for
about 4 minutes to a whipped cream
consistency. Beat in salt and extracts.
Makes 1-1/2 cups frosting.

Hokey-Pokey Cupcakes

A mini version of everyone's favorite poke cake! Make these using any flavor of fruit gelatin you like best. Try using a turkey baster to "spoon" the gelatin over the cupcakes so it's easier to squirt in the holes.

18-1/4 oz. pkg. white cake mix
3-oz. pkg. orange gelatin mix
1 c. boiling water
16-oz. container vanilla frosting
Garnish: candy sprinkles, mini candy-
    coated chocolates, mini jelly beans

Prepare cake mix according to package directions, using egg white version. Fill 24 paper-lined muffin cups; bake as directed. Let cupcakes cool in pans for 15 minutes. Spray a large fork with non-stick vegetable spray; pierce cupcakes with fork at 1/4-inch intervals. Place cupcakes on a paper towel-lined tray and set aside. Add gelatin mix to boiling water, stirring until dissolved; spoon over cupcakes. Chill cupcakes for 3 hours. Frost and garnish as desired. Makes 2 dozen cupcakes.

Fresh-Squeezed Lemonade

To make juicing easier, roll the lemons on your counter, then microwave briefly.

1-3/4 c. sugar
8 c. cold water, divided
6 to 8 lemons
Garnish: ice cubes, lemon slices

Combine sugar and one cup water in a small saucepan. Bring to a boil; stir until sugar dissolves. Cool to room temperature; chill. Juice lemons to measure 1-1/2 cups juice; remove seeds and strain pulp, if desired. In a large pitcher, stir together chilled syrup, juice and remaining water. Chill for several hours to blend flavors. Serve over ice cubes; garnish with additional lemon slices. Makes about 2 quarts, or 8 to 10 servings.

A large flea-market-find blackboard makes a terrific bake sale sign...use colorful chalk to let everyone know the name of your organization and the names of all of the treats you have.

Lemony Pecan Bars

Triple-Delight German Chocolate Cake

Three chocolate layers topped with a pecan-coconut frosting...yummy!

18-1/2 oz. pkg. German chocolate
    cake mix
1 c. evaporated milk
1 c. sugar
3 egg yolks, beaten
1/3 c. butter, softened
1-1/2 c. sweetened flaked coconut
1/2 c. chopped pecans

Prepare and bake cake mix according to package directions for 3 greased 8" round cake pans. Turn layers out of pans; cool. Beat together evaporated milk, sugar, egg yolks and butter in a medium saucepan. Cook and stir over low heat for about 10 minutes, until thick. Remove from heat; stir in coconut and pecans. Let frosting cool; frost and assemble cake on a serving plate. Makes 10 to 12 servings.

Rocky Road Bars!

For bake sale success...
• Set a date close to a holiday...shoppers will be tickled to buy lots of goodies they can freeze, then simply pull out of the freezer when time is short.
• Be sure to add a label to each package and tuck a "Thank you" note inside.
• Keep pricing simple... increments of 25 cents are good, and also means making change is easier for you.

Triple-Delight German Chocolate Cake

Luscious Lemon Layer Cake

Creamy lemon frosting tops an impressive 4-layer cake...best served with a tall glass of icy cold milk!

18-1/2 oz. pkg. lemon cake mix
1/2 t. vanilla extract
1/4 t. lemon extract

Prepare cake mix according to package directions, adding extracts to batter. Bake in 4 greased 8" round cake pans. Turn layers out of pans; cool. Frost with Lemon Frosting and assemble cake on a serving plate. Serves 10 to 12.

Lemon Frosting:

3 pasteurized egg whites
1/4 c. cold water
2 c. sugar
1/4 c. light corn syrup
1/2 c. warm water
1-1/2 t. vanilla extract
1 t. lemon extract
several drops yellow food coloring

Combine egg whites and cold water in a small bowl. Beat with an electric mixer on high speed until stiff peaks form, about 4 minutes. Stir together sugar, corn syrup and warm water in a microwave-safe container; microwave on high setting until boiling, 3 to 5 minutes. Let cool for 2 minutes; slowly add to egg white mixture. Beat with electric mixer on high speed for 4 minutes; add food coloring and continue beating to a spreading consistency. Makes about 4 cups frosting.

Chocolatey Rice Pops

*Garnish these yummy treats with sprinkles
or candy in school colors...sure to be a hit!*

3 T. butter
10-oz. pkg. marshmallows
6 to 7 c. crispy rice cereal
12 wooden treat sticks
6-oz. pkg. semi-sweet chocolate chips,
    melted
1/2 c. white chocolate chips, melted
Optional: mini semi-sweet chocolate
    chips

In a large saucepan, melt butter over
low heat. Add marshmallows; cook
and stir until melted. Remove from
heat; stir in cereal until well-coated.
Press evenly into a lightly greased
13"x9" baking pan. Cool slightly; cut
into 12 bars. Insert a stick in each; set
on wax paper to cool. Dip in melted
chocolate to coat; let cool slightly and
drizzle with melted white chocolate.
Immediately sprinkle with mini chips,
if desired. Makes one dozen pops.

Tip: Melt chocolate chips in a double
boiler over hot water, or in a microwave-
safe bowl (microwave on high for
one minute, stir and microwave an
additional 15 seconds as needed).
Stir until smooth.

Sweet Success Trail Mix

*Scoop this crunchy mix into pastry bags
tied closed with lengths of colorful rick rack.*

10-1/2 oz. pkg. bite-size crispy honey
    nut corn & rice cereal squares
8-oz. pkg. candy-coated chocolates
8-oz. pkg. candy corn
9-oz. pkg. raisins
12-oz. jar dry-roasted peanuts

Combine all ingredients together in
a large bowl; toss to mix. Store in
an airtight container. Makes about
3 pounds.

*Keep bake sale packaging creative. Stack
cookies in tall tumblers and add a tag that
reads, "Just add milk!" or layer trail mix treats
in clear pastry bags and tie with lengths of
gingham ribbon in school colors. You can even
display cupcakes on a vintage tiered plant stand!*

Rocky Road Bars

Brownies, chocolate chips, marshmallows and peanuts...need we say more?

22-1/2 oz. pkg. brownie mix with
    chocolate syrup pouch
1/4 c. water
1/3 c. oil
2 eggs
12-oz. pkg. semi-sweet chocolate chips,
    divided
1-1/2 to 2 c. mini marshmallows
1-1/2 c. dry-roasted peanuts, chopped

Grease the bottom only of a 13"x9" baking pan and set aside. Combine brownie mix, syrup pouch, water, oil and eggs; stir until well blended. Mix in one cup chocolate chips; spread in baking pan. Bake at 350 degrees for 30 to 35 minutes, or until a wooden pick inserted 2 inches from side of pan comes out clean. Immediately sprinkle with marshmallows, remaining chocolate chips and peanuts. Cover pan with a baking sheet for 2 to 3 minutes; remove and cool completely. Cut into bars or squares. Store tightly covered. Makes about 2 dozen bars.

6-Layer Bars

6-Layer Bars

To cut bars easily, line the bottom and sides of the baking pan with aluminum foil before layering ingredients. Once the bars have cooled, lift up on the foil edges to remove the bars from the pan, and then place on a cutting board to slice.

1-1/2 c. graham cracker crumbs
1/2 c. butter, melted
14-oz. can sweetened condensed milk
6-oz. pkg. semi-sweet chocolate chips
2 c. candy-coated chocolates
1-1/3 c. sweetened flaked coconut
1 c. chopped walnuts or pecans

Combine crumbs and butter in a bowl. Mix well and press firmly into the bottom of a lightly greased 13"x9" baking pan. Pour condensed milk evenly over crumb mixture. Sprinkle remaining ingredients evenly over top; press down firmly with a fork. Bake at 350 degrees for 25 minutes, or until lightly golden. Chill; cut into bars or diamonds. Cover and store at room temperature. Makes 2 to 3 dozen bars.

Variations:

Instead of the candy-coated chocolates, use a 6-ounce package of butterscotch chips or a 10-ounce jar of maraschino cherries, drained and chopped.

Chocolatey Rice Pops

Strawberry Delight Cookies

Lemony Pecan Bars

A hint of tangy lemon in these treat bars will make them a fast favorite!

18-1/2 oz. pkg. lemon cake mix
3/4 c. butter, softened
1-1/4 c. chopped pecans, divided
8-oz. pkg. cream cheese, softened
1 c. brown sugar, packed

Mix together dry cake mix, butter and one cup pecans. Press mixture into the bottom of a greased 13"x9" baking pan. Blend cream cheese and brown sugar and spread over top; sprinkle with remaining pecans. Bake at 350 degrees for 25 to 30 minutes, until lightly golden. Cut into bars. Makes 2 to 3 dozen bars.

Streusel-Topped Raspberry Bars

The streusel topping makes these bars irresistible!

2-1/4 c. all-purpose flour
1 c. sugar
1 c. chopped pecans
1 c. butter, softened
1 egg
3/4 c. raspberry preserves
Garnish: powdered sugar

Combine all ingredients except preserves and powdered sugar in a large bowl. Beat with an electric mixer on low speed for 2 to 3 minutes. Set aside 2 cups of mixture for topping. Press remaining mixture into the bottom of a greased 9"x9" baking pan. Spread preserves over top; sprinkle with reserved mixture. Bake at 350 degrees for 40 to 50 minutes, until lightly golden. Cool completely; cut into bars and sprinkle with powdered sugar. Makes 2 dozen bars.

Peanut Butter Bites

*Before baking, top each cookie with a
mini peanut butter cup or chocolate drop
if you'd like.*

1/2 c. sugar
1/2 c. brown sugar, packed
1/2 c. creamy peanut butter
1/4 c. butter, softened
1/4 c. shortening
1 egg
1-1/4 c. all-purpose flour
1/2 t. baking soda
1/2 t. baking powder
1/4 t. salt

In a large bowl, blend sugars, peanut
butter, butter, shortening and egg.
Stir in remaining ingredients. Chill for
about 2 hours, until firm. Form dough
into one-inch balls; place 1-1/2 inches
apart on ungreased baking sheets.
Flatten balls in a criss-cross pattern
with a fork dipped in sugar. Bake at
375 degrees for 9 to 10 minutes, or
until lightly golden. Cool several
minutes; remove from baking sheets.
Cool on a wire rack. Makes 2-1/2 to
3 dozen cookies.

Strawberry Delight Cookies

*The secret is the cake mix...it makes these
cookies so easy to whip up!*

1/4 c. butter, softened
8-oz. pkg. cream cheese, softened
1 egg
1/4 t. vanilla extract
18-1/2 oz. pkg. strawberry cake mix
3/4 to 1 c. prepared strawberry frosting

Blend together butter and cream
cheese; stir in egg and vanilla. Add
dry cake mix one-third at a time,
mixing well after each addition.
Cover and chill for 30 minutes. Drop
by teaspoonfuls onto ungreased baking
sheets. Bake at 375 degrees for 10 to
12 minutes. Microwave frosting for
15 to 30 seconds; drizzle over cooled
cookies. Makes 4 dozen cookies.

*Dress up plain paper plates in a jiffy...it couldn't
be easier. Use decorative-edged scrapbook
scissors to trim the edges of paper plates. Punch
holes along the edges and weave ribbon through
the holes. Top with your bake sale treats, slip
into cello bags and watch them disappear!*

BIG *

CHOCOLATE CHIP
COOKIES

Banana
Bread

Best-Ever Banana Bread

Big Chocolate Chip Cookies

No one can resist warm, chocolate chip cookies! Stack 3 together and tie up with a gingham bow.

2 c. all-purpose flour
1/2 t. baking soda
1/2 t. salt
3/4 c. butter, melted
1 c. brown sugar, packed
1/2 c. sugar
1 egg
1 egg yolk
1 T. vanilla extract
12-oz. pkg. semi-sweet chocolate chips

Combine flour, baking soda and salt in a medium bowl; mix well and set aside. In a large bowl, beat together butter and sugars until well blended. Add egg, egg yolk and vanilla; beat until light and creamy. Add flour mixture; stir until just blended. Stir in chocolate chips by hand. Form dough into balls, 1/4 cup at a time; arrange 2 inches apart on greased or parchment paper-lined baking sheets. Bake at 325 degrees for 15 to 17 minutes, or until edges are golden. Cool on baking sheets for several minutes; cool on a wire rack. Makes about 15 cookies.

Best-Ever Banana Bread

You can also spoon the batter into a 9"x9" baking pan and cut into squares for a tasty snack cake.

1/2 c. shortening
1 c. sugar
2 eggs
3/4 c. ripe banana, mashed
1-1/4 c. cake flour, sifted
3/4 c. baking soda
1/2 t. salt

In a large mixing bowl, blend shortening and sugar well. Add eggs, one at a time, beating well after each; stir in banana and set aside. Stir together flour, baking soda and salt in a separate bowl; add to shortening mixture and mix well. Pour into 6 greased 5-1/2"x3" mini loaf pans. Bake at 350 degrees for 40 to 45 minutes. Makes 6 mini loaves.

If your bake sale is outdoors, be sure to set up under a canopy just in case the weather changes. Just for fun, top your display tables with a few canning jars of perky blossoms, or vintage soda bottles filled with a cheery sunflower.

picnic *bbq*

Greek Pasta Salad

Calico Beans

Summertime joys...

school is out and the pools are open. We can hardly wait for summer and all that comes with it...parades and picnics, sparklers and strawberries, fireflies and flashlight tag. When the calendar turns to July, the heart of summer has arrived.

On the 4th of July, we gather with friends & neighbors to celebrate Independence Day. Whether we're in a big city or a small town, patriotism is in full swing...from flags waving in the warm summer breeze to buntings dressing up porches. A barbecue is a sure-fire way to bring everyone together before dusk falls and the annual fireworks spectacular begins.

We've kept the menu easy while taking in the best summer has to offer. Grilled Sweet Corn topped with tangy Lime-Chive Butter is a must-have. Country-Style Baby Back Ribs are fall-off-the-bone tender and Dilly Blue Cheese Potato Salad can be made the night before. Slices of Very Berry Peach Pie topped with scoops of Old-Fashioned Vanilla Ice Cream (homemade!) will disappear quickly.

Summer celebrations...a time best shared with family & friends enjoying the simple pleasures in this country that we love.

GRILLED SWEET CORN
WITH LIME-CHIVE BUTTER

CALICO BEANS

DILLY BLUE CHEESE POTATO SALAD

GREEK PASTA SALAD

ZESTY APPLE SLAW

SMOKEY BACON-GOUDA BURGERS

BRIE-STUFFED BURGERS

COUNTRY-STYLE BABY BACK RIBS

OLD-FASHIONED VANILLA
ICE CREAM

SODA SHOPPE ROOT BEER FLOATS

MOM'S LEMON ICEBOX PIE

SUMMERTIME STRAWBERRY
SHORTCAKE

VERY BERRY PEACH PIE

Dilly Blue Cheese Potato Salad

Keep summertime decorating full of patriotic whimsy. Fill glass canning jars with red, white & blue buttons, cool water and some perky garden blooms, or do something completely unexpected... arrange several flags inside a pair of red cowboy boots!

Grilled Sweet Corn with Lime-Chive Butter

A summertime must-have takes on a new taste when grilled and topped with flavorful Lime-Chive Butter!

8 ears sweet corn in husks
Garnish: Lime-Chive Butter

Gently pull back corn husks and remove corn silk; press husks back into place. Soak corn in ice water for 30 minutes; drain well. Grill over medium to medium-high heat for 15 to 20 minutes, turning occasionally, until husks are charred and corn is tender. Serve with Lime-Chive Butter. Makes 8 servings.

Lime-Chive Butter:

1/2 c. butter, softened
1/3 c. fresh chives, finely chopped
2 t. lime juice
1 t. lime zest
1/2 t. salt
1/4 t. paprika
1/8 t. cayenne pepper

Blend together all ingredients; chill. Makes about 2/3 cup.

Grilled Sweet Corn
with Lime-Chive Butter

Calico Beans

This 5-bean bake is a traditional side dish...no cookout would be complete without it.

12-oz. pkg. bacon, cut into 1-inch
    pieces
1/2 c. onion, chopped
28-oz. can pork & beans
15-oz. can barbecue beans
15-oz. can kidney beans, drained and
    rinsed
15-1/2 oz. can butter beans, drained
    and rinsed
16-oz. can navy beans, drained and
    rinsed
3/4 c. brown sugar, packed
1/2 c. white vinegar
1 t. dry mustard
1 t. garlic salt

Cook bacon in a skillet until crisp.
Drain on paper towels, reserving
drippings in skillet. Sauté onion in
reserved drippings until tender, about
4 minutes. Combine onion mixture,
bacon and remaining ingredients in a
greased 3-quart casserole dish. Bake,
uncovered, at 350 degrees for 2 hours.
Makes 20 servings.

Picnic

Dilly Blue Cheese Potato Salad

Try this new spin on potato salad...redskin potatoes combined with tangy blue cheese and sour cream.

1 c. mayonnaise
1 c. sour cream
2 t. lemon juice
1 bunch green onions, chopped
5 stalks celery, chopped
1/2 c. fresh dill, chopped
1/2 c. crumbled blue cheese
3 lbs. new redskin potatoes, quartered
    and cooked
1 t. salt
pepper to taste

Blend together mayonnaise, sour cream
and lemon juice in a large bowl. Add
onions, celery and dill; fold in blue
cheese and potatoes. Add salt and
pepper to taste. Chill overnight. Makes
10 servings.

bbq

Greek Pasta Salad

Penne or bowtie pasta work equally well in this classic recipe, as do whole black olives.

3 c. cooked elbow macaroni
3 c. sliced mushrooms, diced
15 cherry tomatoes, halved
1 c. yellow or red pepper, sliced
1/2 c. green onion, chopped
3/4 c. sliced black olives, drained
1 c. crumbled feta cheese
Optional: 3/4 c. pepperoni, diced
1/2 c. olive oil
1/2 c. red wine vinegar
1-1/2 t. garlic powder
1-1/2 t. dried basil
1-1/2 t. dried oregano
3/4 t. pepper
3/4 t. sugar

In a large bowl, combine macaroni, vegetables, cheese and pepperoni, if using; set aside. Whisk together remaining ingredients in a small bowl. Pour over macaroni mixture and toss until evenly coated. Cover and chill 2 hours to overnight. Makes 10 to 12 servings.

Zesty Apple Slaw

With its fresh, crisp taste, you'll be asked to share this recipe!

1/2 head red cabbage, finely shredded
1/4 c. onion, finely chopped
2 Fuji apples, cored, peeled and finely diced
1 c. mayonnaise
1/2 t. salt
1/8 t. pepper
2 t. sugar
2 T. lemon juice
2 T. milk

Toss together cabbage, onion and apples in a large bowl; set aside. Whisk together remaining ingredients in a small bowl; toss with cabbage mixture. Chill until serving time. Makes 6 servings.

Bottles of cream soda, root beer or lemonade get a fanciful look when wrapped in colorful paper and topped off with a tag and bow. How fun!

Smokey Bacon-Gouda Burgers

Not your ordinary burgers on the grill... we flavor ours with a dash of hot pepper sauce, a bacon-onion mixture and spicy steak seasoning.

1/4 c. onion, finely chopped
6 slices bacon, cut into 1/2-inch pieces, crisply cooked and 1 T. drippings reserved
1/4 c. onion, finely chopped
2 T. olive oil
1-3/4 c. onion, thinly sliced
1/4 c. steak sauce
1-1/2 lbs. ground beef sirloin
2 t. Worcestershire sauce
1 t. hot pepper sauce
1 T. grill steak seasoning
4 slices smoked Gouda cheese
4 kaiser rolls or onion rolls, split and toasted
Optional: crisply cooked bacon, sliced tomato, lettuce leaves

In a skillet over medium heat, cook chopped onion in reserved drippings until soft, 2 to 3 minutes. Combine with bacon in a small bowl; set aside. Heat oil in skillet; add sliced onion and sauté, covered, until golden, about 10 minutes. Place in another bowl; stir in steak sauce and set aside. In a large bowl, combine ground beef, remaining sauces, steak seasoning and onion-bacon mixture; mix lightly and form into 4 patties. Grill over medium-high heat to desired doneness, 4 to 6 minutes per side, topping with cheese slices when nearly done. Serve burgers on toasted rolls, topped with sliced onion mixture and with extra crisply cooked bacon, tomato and lettuce, if desired. Makes 4 servings.

Variations:

Red Pepper & Jack Burgers:

Prepare burgers as directed, adding one to 2 cloves minced garlic to ground beef mixture. Form into 8 thin patties. Place a slice of Monterey Jack cheese on each of 4 patties; top with remaining patties and press to seal. Grill as directed. Serve burgers on onion rolls, topped with thinly sliced red onion, roasted red peppers and sliced avocado.

Mushroom & Swiss Burgers:

Prepare and grill 4 burgers as directed. For topping, replace onion with sliced mushrooms; sauté as directed. Top burgers with Swiss cheese slices and sautéed mushrooms.

Smokey Bacon-Gouda Burgers

Very Berry Peach Pie

Country-Style Baby Back Ribs

Brie-Stuffed Burgers

Ground turkey makes an excellent, moist burger when grilled. With a cube of Brie cheese inside and smothered with grilled apples, these burgers are amazing!

2 lbs. ground turkey
6 cubes Brie cheese, 1"x1"x1/2"
2 T. olive oil, divided
salt and pepper to taste
1 tart apple, cored and thickly sliced
  crosswise
6 multi-grain rolls, split and toasted
Optional: cranberry mustard

Form turkey into 6 thick patties. Hollow out center of each and place a cheese cube inside; press meat around cheese to cover. Brush one tablespoon oil over burgers; sprinkle to taste with salt and pepper. Grill over medium-high heat to desired doneness. Brush remaining oil over apple slices; grill (or sauté in a skillet) until golden. Place burgers on rolls; top with apple slices and a dollop of cranberry mustard, if desired. Makes 6 servings.

Country-Style Baby Back Ribs

Grilled until tender and brushed with a brown sugar sauce, these juicy ribs are sure to please everyone.

3 lbs. baby back pork ribs, cut into
    serving-size pieces
2 T. olive oil
1 onion, chopped
1 stalk celery, chopped
1 clove garlic, minced
1 c. catsup
1/4 c. brown sugar, packed
1/4 c. red wine vinegar
2 T. Worcestershire sauce
1 T. Dijon mustard

Fill a large stockpot with water; bring to a boil over medium-high heat. Add ribs; reduce heat, cover and simmer for 40 minutes. Remove ribs and pat dry with paper towels; place in a shallow pan and set aside. To make sauce, heat oil in a medium saucepan. Sauté onion, celery and garlic over medium heat until tender, about 5 minutes. Add remaining ingredients; simmer for 10 minutes, stirring occasionally. Transfer mixture to a food processor. Process until smooth, about one minute. Reserve 1/2 cup sauce for serving with ribs; brush ribs with one cup remaining sauce. Cover ribs; chill for 30 minutes. Grill over medium-high heat for 5 minutes per side, until slightly blackened and heated through. Reduce heat to low; brush ribs with additional sauce and grill for 15 minutes. Turn ribs and grill an additional 15 minutes, brushing with sauce. Serve with reserved sauce. Makes 4 servings.

The roomy size of a vintage metal cooler makes it perfect for loading with ice and watermelon, or stock it with bottled water, sodas and juice boxes.

Old-Fashioned Vanilla Ice Cream

It's really easy to make your own homemade ice cream, and the flavor is unbelievable!

2 qts. half-and-half
1 c. whipping cream
1-1/2 c. sugar
4 t. vanilla extract
1/8 t. salt

Combine all ingredients in a large pitcher; stir until sugar is dissolved. Pour into a 4 or 5-quart ice cream maker; freeze according to manufacturer's instructions. Serve immediately or transfer to a freezer-safe container and store in freezer for several hours. Makes 4 quarts.

Variations:

Peach or Strawberry Ice Cream:

Lightly mash 2 cups sliced ripe fruit with 1/4 cup sugar; stir into unfrozen ice cream mixture. Pour into ice cream maker and freeze as directed.

Chocolate-Pecan Ice Cream:

Prepare ice cream as directed. Stir in 1/2 cup caramel ice cream topping; store ice cream in freezer. Place one cup semi-sweet chocolate chips and 2 teaspoons shortening in a microwave-safe bowl. Microwave on high setting one minute; stir until smooth. Drizzle over 1-1/2 cups chopped pecans on a parchment paper-lined baking sheet. Freeze 5 minutes; break into bite-size pieces and stir into ice cream.

bbg

Soda Shoppe Root Beer Floats

This frosty delight is something we all grew up loving!

1 pt. vanilla ice cream
2 12-oz. bottles root beer, chilled
1 c. whipped topping
Optional: 4 maraschino cherries

Place one scoop ice cream into each of 4 tall glasses. Pour root beer slowly over top. Add another scoop and repeat. Garnish each glass with a dollop of whipped topping and a cherry, if desired. Serves 4.

Mom's Lemon Icebox Pie

A cool, old-fashioned treat to beat the summer heat.

1-1/2 c. vanilla wafers, finely crushed
1/4 c. butter, melted
14-oz. can sweetened condensed milk
1/2 c. lemon juice
Optional: few drops yellow food
    coloring
1 c. whipping cream, whipped

Stir together vanilla wafer crumbs and butter. Press firmly into an ungreased 9" pie plate; chill. In a medium bowl, stir together condensed milk, lemon juice and food coloring, if using. Fold in whipped cream; pour into chilled crust. Chill for 3 hours, or until set. Makes 6 to 8 servings.

Relive the fun of summertime favorites... Red Rover, 3-legged races, water balloons, horseshoes, freeze tag and bike parades!

*Summertime Strawberry Shortcake
and Mom's Lemon Icebox Pie*

Summertime Strawberry Shortcake

One dessert you'll want to make when fresh strawberries are in season...so sweet & simple.

3 to 4 c. strawberries, hulled and sliced
1/2 c. plus 2 T. sugar, divided
2 c. all-purpose flour
1 T. baking powder
1/2 t. salt
3/4 c. butter, divided
1 egg, beaten
2/3 c. light cream
1 c. whipping cream, whipped

Toss strawberries with 1/2 cup sugar and set aside. Combine flour, remaining sugar, baking powder and salt in a medium bowl. Cut in 1/2 cup butter until mixture forms coarse crumbs; set aside. Whisk together egg and light cream in a small bowl. Add to flour mixture, stirring just until moistened; pat into a greased 8" round cake pan. Bake at 450 degrees for 15 to 18 minutes, until golden. Turn out of pan and cool on a wire rack for several minutes. With a serrated knife, split cake in half horizontally and carefully lift off top. Spread remaining softened butter over bottom layer. Spoon half of berries and whipped cream over bottom layer; add top layer. Top with remaining berries and cream. Cut into wedges to serve. Makes 6 servings.

Very Berry Peach Pie

For a tasty twist, bake pie, then layer
servings with ice cream in sundae cups.

2 9-inch pie crusts
4 c. peaches, pitted, peeled and sliced
1-1/2 c. blackberries
1 c. blueberries
3/4 c. plus 2 t. sugar, divided
1/4 c. all-purpose flour
2 T. butter, diced

Line a 9" pie plate with one crust
and set aside. Combine fruit in a large
bowl; mix gently. Blend 3/4 cup sugar
and flour in a small bowl; toss lightly
with fruit mixture. Pour fruit mixture
into prepared crust; dot with butter.
Cover with remaining crust; trim and
crimp edges. Cut vents in crust; cover
edge of crust with strips of aluminum
foil to prevent overbrowning. Bake at
425 degrees for 35 to 40 minutes, until
golden. Makes 6 to 8 servings.

Soda Shoppe Root Beer Floats

recipe *swap*

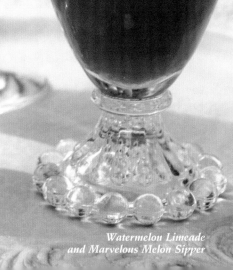

*Watermelon Limeade
and Marvelous Melon Sipper*

Fresh Fruit Kabobs with Poppyseed Dip

Welcome friends

to a recipe swap! A sunny weekend afternoon is the perfect time to get together to share tried & true recipes. You know the ones...those that are just right for special occasions and the "must-haves" for family reunions. The ones you reach for time & time again.

Drop invitations in the mail so friends have plenty of time to sort through their recipes and pull out 5 of their favorites to share. Ask them to make enough copies for each person who will be coming, and even bring along their best-loved dish to share at a potluck lunch. All you need to do is set up a table outside in the garden where everyone can enjoy a warm breeze or just sit in the porch swing while catching up.

To make our "must-have" recipes, a trip to the farmers' market will produce an armload of homegrown fruits & vegetables that practically prepare themselves. We love the delicious combination of Minted Asparagus Slaw, Grilled Salmon Quesadillas with Roasted Corn Salsa and crispy, golden Fried Green Tomatoes.

After lunch, settle in to share stories of how your favorite recipes came to be...you'll find each has a sweet memory all its own.

CHILLED AVOCADO-TOMATO SOUP

3-CHEESE ARTICHOKE BITES

FRIED GREEN TOMATOES WITH ROASTED RED PEPPER SAUCE

GRILLED CORN & SHRIMP SALAD

MINTED ASPARAGUS SLAW

CHICKEN & CHEDDAR PURSES

GOLDEN CRAB CAKES

GRILLED SALMON QUESADILLAS WITH ROASTED CORN SALSA

WATERMELON LIMEADE

MARVELOUS MELON SIPPER

FRESH FRUIT KABOBS WITH POPPYSEED DIP

GOLDEN TEQUILA LIME TART

Chilled Avocado-Tomato Soup

Refreshing and full of flavor…ideal for a warm-weather supper. Tangy sourdough or rosemary rolls are just right served alongside.

2 lbs. ripe tomatoes, chopped
3 to 4 T. white wine vinegar
salt to taste
2 avocados, pitted, peeled and chopped
3/4 c. chicken broth
1/4 c. sour cream
3 T. lime juice
1 cucumber, peeled and diced
3 T. shallots, minced
1 t. fresh basil or tarragon, minced

Purée tomatoes in a blender until smooth. Press through a colander, discarding pulp remaining in colander. Place tomato purée in a bowl; add vinegar and salt to taste and set aside.

Purée avocados, broth, sour cream and lime juice in blender until smooth; add salt to taste and set aside. Combine cucumber, shallots and basil or tarragon in a small bowl; chill all 3 mixtures for one hour. At serving time, stir each mixture separately to blend. Divide avocado purée among 6 to 8 clear glasses or bowls; gently spoon tomato purée over top. Garnish with cucumber mixture. Serves 6 to 8.

Chilled Avocado-Tomato Soup

3-Cheese Artichoke Bites

Bite-size appetizers filled with Cheddar, mozzarella and Parmesan cheeses...scrumptious!

1 onion, chopped
1 clove garlic, minced
1 T. oil
2 6-1/2 oz. jars marinated artichokes,
    drained and chopped
6 eggs, beaten
1 c. shredded Cheddar cheese
1 c. shredded mozzarella cheese
1 c. grated Parmesan cheese
1/2 t. Italian seasoning
1/4 c. fresh parsley, chopped
1/4 t. pepper
1/8 t. Worcestershire sauce
1/8 t. hot pepper sauce
1/4 c. Italian-seasoned dry bread
    crumbs

In a skillet over medium heat, sauté onion and garlic in oil until tender; drain and set aside. Combine artichokes, eggs, cheeses, seasonings and sauces in a large bowl and mix well. Stir in onion mixture and bread crumbs. Fill greased mini muffin tins 2/3 full. Bake at 325 degrees for 15 to 20 minutes, until firm and golden. Serve warm. Makes 3-1/2 to 4 dozen.

Fried Green Tomatoes with Roasted Red Pepper Sauce

For a thicker, crunchier coating, dip tomato slices a second time in buttermilk and cornmeal mixture before cooking.

1-1/2 c. buttermilk
salt and pepper to taste
1 c. cornmeal
1 c. all-purpose flour
1 T. garlic powder
1/8 t. cayenne pepper
4 to 5 green tomatoes, sliced
1/2 c. oil
1 T. butter

Pour buttermilk into a shallow bowl. Add salt and pepper to taste; set aside. Mix cornmeal, flour, garlic powder and cayenne pepper in a second shallow bowl. Dip tomato slices into buttermilk and then into cornmeal mixture, coating well on both sides. Heat oil in a large cast iron skillet over medium heat. Cook tomato slices in batches until crisp and golden, 3 to 4 minutes on each side. Drain on paper towels; serve hot with Roasted Red Pepper Sauce for dipping. Makes 4 to 8 servings.

Roasted Red Pepper Sauce:

2 c. mayonnaise
1 c. roasted red peppers, drained
1/2 c. olive oil
3/4 t. celery salt
3/4 t. pepper
1-1/2 T. hot pepper sauce
1-1/2 T. lemon juice

Purée mayonnaise and red peppers together in a blender or food processor. Slowly add oil, blending until well mixed. Stir in remaining ingredients; chill for one hour. Stir before serving. Makes 3 cups.

recipe

swap

Grilled Corn & Shrimp Salad

If you'd like a bolder flavor, before grilling corn, brush the kernels with olive oil, lime juice and fresh cilantro to taste.

2 ears corn, husked
1 t. chili sauce
1/2 t. ground cumin
1/2 t. salt
1/4 t. pepper
2 lbs. uncooked large shrimp, peeled
    and cleaned
3 T. olive oil, divided
2 to 3 tomatoes, cut into thin wedges
1/2 cucumber, halved lengthwise and
    thinly sliced
8 c. spring mix greens
1 avocado, pitted, peeled and thinly
    sliced
Garnish: 2 T. fresh mint, thinly sliced

Grill or broil corn for about 5 minutes, until slightly browned but not burnt. Cool; slice off kernels and set aside. Stir together chili sauce, cumin, salt and pepper in a large bowl. Add shrimp; toss to coat. Heat 2 tablespoons oil in a large skillet over high heat. Add half of shrimp; sauté until no longer pink, about 3 minutes. Remove cooked shrimp to another large bowl; set aside. Add remaining oil to skillet; sauté remaining shrimp. Cool. Add shrimp to bowl; stir in corn kernels, tomatoes and cucumber. Chill. At serving time, arrange greens on a serving platter. Top with shrimp mixture and avocado. Drizzle with dressing; sprinkle with mint. Makes 8 to 10 servings.

Dressing:

1/4 c. olive oil
2 T. plus 2 t. lime juice
4 t. soy sauce
2 t. toasted sesame oil
1/4 t. pepper

Whisk all ingredients together; chill.

Be on the lookout for vintage tin lunchboxes, child-size sandpails or bicycle baskets at tag sales and flea markets...all whimsical ways to keep recipes organized and at your fingertips.

With some scrapbooking papers, stickers, scissors and tags, you and your friends can make the sweetest recipe books in no time! Invite each friend to bring enough copies of her recipe on cards to share. Use your imagination to create whimsical front & back book covers, then punch holes across the tops of all recipe cards and covers. Secure books with lengths of jute and you're done! A sweet reminder of a day spent with friends.

Minted Asparagus Slaw

Fresh herbs and crisp vegetables really give this dish its flavor. On days when time is short, buy bags of pre-shredded cabbage from the market.

1 lb. asparagus, trimmed and cut into
    4-inch lengths
4 c. green cabbage, shredded
1 c. red cabbage, shredded
1/2 c. carrot, peeled and finely shredded
2 to 3 T. red onion, thinly sliced
1/4 c. fresh mint, chopped
1/4 c. fresh parsley, chopped
Garnish: lemon slices

Bring one inch water to a boil in a medium saucepan. Add asparagus in a steamer basket; cover and steam until crisp-tender, 4 to 6 minutes. Drain; rinse with cold water and chill. Combine cabbages, carrot, onion and herbs in a large bowl; add dressing and toss lightly. Chill for several hours to overnight. To serve, toss cabbage mixture with dressing and spoon into salad bowls or clear glass tumblers. Tuck several asparagus spears into each serving; garnish with lemon slices. Makes 8 to 10 servings.

Dressing:

2 T. olive oil
2 T. balsamic vinegar
1 T. lemon juice
1 T. lemon zest
1 clove garlic, minced
1/2 t. pepper

Place all ingredients in a lidded jar; cover and shake well.

Minted Asparagus Slaw

Grilled Corn &
Shrimp Salad

Chicken & Cheddar
Purses

Chicken & Cheddar Purses

For an extra-special garnish, tie a green onion top around the filled puff pastry twists after baking.

1-1/4 c. cooked chicken, diced
1 c. shredded Cheddar cheese
3-oz. pkg. cream cheese, softened
3 T. mayonnaise
1/4 c. celery, thinly sliced
1/4 c. green onion, sliced
1 T. pimento, chopped
1/2 t. garlic salt
1/8 t. pepper
17.3-oz. pkg. frozen puff pastry,
    thawed
1 egg
1 T. water

Mix together all ingredients except pastry, egg and water; set aside. Unfold thawed pastry on a lightly floured surface. Roll each sheet into a 12"x12" square. Cut six, 6"x6" squares, reserving remaining pastry for another use. Spoon 1/3 cup chicken mixture onto center of each square. Bring 4 corners of pastry to center; twist slightly and press edges to seal, forming a bundle shape. Arrange bundles on an ungreased baking sheet. Whisk together egg and water; brush over bundles. Bake at 400 degrees for 15 to 25 minutes, until golden. Makes 6 servings.

Golden Crab Cakes

Not only delectable, but so simple to make. You'll find the Roasted Red Pepper Sauce on page 96 is a great go-with!

3 c. saltine cracker crumbs, divided
2 eggs, beaten
1/2 c. onion, diced
3 T. mayonnaise
1 T. mustard
2 t. lemon juice
1/2 t. salt
1/4 t. pepper
1/8 t. cayenne pepper
1/4 t. hot pepper sauce
1 lb. refrigerated fresh lump crabmeat
2 T. butter
2 T. oil

Stir together 2 cups cracker crumbs, eggs, onion, mayonnaise, mustard, lemon juice and seasonings; fold in crabmeat. Shape into eight, 3-inch patties; dredge in remaining crumbs. In a large skillet over medium-high heat, melt butter and oil together. Cook crab cakes until golden, about 4 minutes on each side. Makes 8 servings.

A tisket, a tasket...a wicker picnic basket is a must for a morning spent at the farmers' market. It has to be roomy enough to handle a peck of peppers or bouquet of blooms...you never know what you might want to bring home!

Grilled Salmon Quesadillas with Roasted Corn Salsa

A variety of flavorful flour tortillas is nice for this recipe. Try using tortillas flavored with sun-dried tomatoes, spinach-herb or chipotle chiles.

1/2 lb. salmon fillet, 3/4-inch thick
8 6-inch flour tortillas
1 c. shredded Monterey Jack cheese
1/2 c. shredded Cheddar cheese
1/4 to 1/2 c. butter

Place salmon on a grill over medium-high heat. Cover and grill for 5 minutes on each side, until fish flakes easily. Let cool; flake with a fork. Divide salmon and cheeses among 4 tortillas; top with remaining tortillas. Melt butter in a large non-stick skillet over high heat. Cook quesadillas, one at a time, until lightly golden and cheese is melted. Cut each into quarters; serve with Roasted Corn Salsa. Makes 16 wedges.

Roasted Corn Salsa:

3 ears corn, husked
1 red pepper, diced
1 red onion, diced
1 jalapeño pepper, seeded and minced
2 tomatoes, diced
1/2 bunch fresh cilantro, chopped
1/2 c. red wine vinegar
2 T. olive oil

Grill or broil corn for about 5 minutes, just until slightly browned. Cool; slice off kernels. Toss with remaining ingredients in a small bowl; chill.

swap

Watermelon Limeade

*Sweet, tangy, frosty...a super
thirst quencher!*

3 c. watermelon, cubed and seeded
4 c. water
1/4 c. sugar
1/4 c. lime juice
crushed ice
Garnish: fresh mint sprigs or
    mini watermelon wedges

Place watermelon cubes in a blender;
blend until smooth. Combine with
water, sugar and lime juice in a pitcher;
chill. Serve over ice, garnished with
sprigs of fresh mint or skewers of mini
watermelon wedges. Makes 6 servings.

Marvelous Melon Sipper

*Melon, lime and mint...a refreshing
summertime drink that's a sure-fire winner.*

6 c. honeydew melon, cubed and
    seeded
1-1/2 c. sugar
1-3/4 c. lime juice
3 T. fresh mint, chopped
3 c. water
crushed ice
Optional: melon balls

Working in batches, process honeydew
cubes, sugar, lime juice and mint in a
blender until smooth. Pour into a
pitcher; chill. Serve over ice, garnished
with skewers of melon balls, if desired.
Makes 10 to 12 servings.

*Tuck posies into colorful 1950's jelly
glasses...they make charming take-home
gifts for friends.*

103

Golden Tequila Lime Tart

Fresh Fruit Kabobs with Poppyseed Dip

For a new spin, you can also try grilling fresh fruit kabobs. Brush the grill rack lightly with oil, and grill over medium-high heat for 3 to 5 minutes...so delicious!

6 c. fresh fruit like strawberries, kiwi, pineapple, honeydew, cantaloupe, peeled and cut into bite-size pieces
6 to 8 wooden skewers
1/2 c. vanilla yogurt
1 T. honey
2 t. lime juice
1/2 t. vanilla extract
1/2 t. poppyseed

Arrange fruit cubes and slices alternately on skewers. For Poppyseed Dip, stir together remaining ingredients in a small bowl. Serve dip alongside fruit kabobs. Makes 6 to 8 servings.

───── ❦ ─────

Share a bottle of rosemary or chive vinegar with friends as a "thanks for coming" gift. Summer's herbal vinegars steeped in pretty glass bottles add a zesty flavor splashed on salads or over grilled veggies. Simply add several sprigs of freshly picked, washed and dried herbs to a sterilized jar. Fill the jar with white wine vinegar. Seal the jar (if you can't avoid a metal lid, place plastic on the top of the jar before adding the lid) and set aside for 4 to 6 weeks so the herbs can blend into the vinegar.

Golden Tequila Lime Tart

If using a 9-1/2" tart pan, the filling will be mounded, but won't overflow while baking. The center will bake up puffy and golden.

12 graham crackers
1/4 c. pine nuts
3 T. sugar, divided
1/2 c. butter, melted
14-oz. can sweetened condensed milk
1/2 c. lime juice
1/4 c. gold tequila
4 egg yolks
2 egg whites
Garnish: whipped cream, lime slices

Crush graham crackers; process finely in a food processor. Measure out 1-1/2 cups; set aside in a medium bowl. Finely grind nuts and 2 tablespoons sugar in food processor; stir nut mixture and butter into crumbs. Press mixture evenly onto bottom and up sides of an ungreased 9"x9" baking pan; set aside. In a large bowl, whisk together condensed milk, lime juice, tequila and egg yolks until well blended. In another large bowl, beat egg whites and remaining sugar with an electric mixer on high speed until soft peaks form. Stir one-quarter of egg white mixture into condensed milk mixture; gently fold in remaining egg white mixture until thoroughly combined. Spoon filling into crust. Bake at 325 degrees for 25 to 30 minutes, until edges of filling are puffed and light golden, and center is set. Cool completely on a wire rack; cover loosely and chill for 2 hours to overnight. Cut into small squares; garnish as desired. Makes about 24 servings.

Serve up fun at your garden lunch...a new watering can makes a terrific pitcher for our Marvelous Melon Sipper or Watermelon Limeade.

tag *sale*

Classic Tuna Noodle Casserole

Cherry Delight Cobbler

"*Let's go antiquing!*" These three little words can quicken the pulse like nothing else! We love vintage metal lawn furniture, cheery kitchenware and anything handmade and painted. However, the next best thing to spotting a "must-have" at a tag sale is to host your own sale with friends. Invite friends to look through boxes tucked in attics and stored in barns, and then tote their "treasures" to your home for a day filled with fun!

Catch the attention of passersby...an old chalkboard or metal flea market sign is ideal. A vintage tin recipe box makes a handy cash box and a Mason jar is just right for holding tags, scissors, markers and jute for tagging sale items. The kids can even set up a lemonade stand...our recipe for Chamomile Cooler is so refreshing!

After a day of swapping trinkets and tales, you'll want to sit down and enjoy dinner together. Add whimsy by using school lunch trays topped with Shredded Chicken Sandwiches, Classic Tuna Noodle Casserole and a side of Frosty Fruit Salad or Cherry Delight Cobbler. Fill glass milk bottles with icy sodas, tie up silverware in a napkin and top off with a length of rick rack. Then sit back and relax...it's been a great day!

BBQ Nachos

Leftover, homemade pulled pork or shredded chicken is delicious too...just add a cup or so of your favorite BBQ sauce to two cups of meat.

20-oz. container shredded pork in
   barbecue sauce
16-oz. can refried beans
2 T. lime juice
Cajun seasoning to taste
2 tomatoes, coarsely chopped
1 onion, chopped
1/2 c. sliced jalapeño peppers
1/2 c. fresh cilantro, chopped
7-oz. pkg. white corn tortilla chips,
   divided
1/3 c. sour cream
12-oz. pkg. shredded Cheddar cheese
Garnish: sour cream, fresh cilantro

Microwave pork in barbecue sauce on high setting until heated through; stir and set aside. In a small bowl, mix beans, lime juice and seasoning; set aside. In another small bowl, combine tomatoes, onion, jalapeños and cilantro. Arrange half of tortilla chips in an ungreased 13"x9" baking pan; top with spoonfuls of pork, bean mixture, sour cream and half of tomato mixture. Arrange remaining chips on top; spoon remaining tomato mixture over chips. If desired, drizzle with any barbecue sauce remaining from pork. Sprinkle to taste with additional Cajun seasoning; top with shredded cheese. Placing oven rack 6 inches below broiler, broil nachos for 5 to 7 minutes, until cheese melts and begins to turn golden. Garnish with additional sour cream and cilantro. Makes 6 to 8 servings.

Out-of-this-World Corn Dip

This lives up to its name...here at
Gooseberry Patch *we have it at every*
gathering!

3 11-oz. cans sweet corn & diced
   peppers, drained
7-oz. can chopped green chiles
6-oz. can chopped jalapeño peppers,
   drained and liquid added to taste
1/2 c. green onion, chopped
1 c. mayonnaise
1 c. sour cream
1 t. pepper
1/2 t. garlic powder
16-oz. pkg. shredded sharp
   Cheddar cheese
scoop-type corn chips

In a large bowl, mix all ingredients
except chips. Chill 2 hours to
overnight. Serve with corn chips
for scooping. Makes 6 cups.

Frosty Fruit Salad

Absolutely sure to please...add this frozen,
fruity salad to the buffet table and watch
it disappear.

16-oz. pkg. frozen sliced strawberries,
   partially thawed
12-oz. can frozen orange juice
   concentrate, partially thawed
2 15-oz. cans fruit cocktail in syrup
20-oz. can crushed pineapple in juice
3 bananas, diced

Mix together all ingredients, including
juices from fruit. Pour into a 13"x9"
plastic freezer container; cover and
freeze. To serve, let stand at room
temperature for 30 to 40 minutes.
Scoop out portions with a small ice
cream scoop. Makes 32 servings.

Make your own price tags...quick & easy with
office supply shipping tags! Use pinking shears
to trim the bottom edge and just tie on. If you
want tags that look old, sponge on strong tea
or coffee, let dry, then mark up and tie on.

Panzanella Salad

The simple combination of bread with garden-fresh ingredients becomes a savory salad.

1/2 c. olive oil, divided
1 loaf French bread, cut into
    1-inch cubes
1 t. salt
2 to 3 ripe tomatoes, cut into
    1-inch cubes
1 red pepper, cut into 1-inch cubes
1 yellow pepper, cut into 1-inch cubes
1 cucumber, sliced 1/2-inch thick
1/2 red onion, halved and thinly sliced
1 bunch fresh basil, coarsely chopped
3 T. capers
Optional: salt and pepper to taste

Heat 2 tablespoons oil over low to medium heat in a large skillet. Add bread and salt to skillet; sauté until deep golden, about 10 minutes, tossing frequently and adding remaining oil as needed. Drain on paper towels. Mix remaining ingredients except salt and pepper in a large salad bowl; add bread. Drizzle with vinaigrette and toss; add salt and pepper to taste, if desired. Let stand for 30 minutes before serving. Makes 12 servings.

Vinaigrette:

1 t. garlic, minced
1/2 t. Dijon mustard
3 T. champagne vinegar
1/2 c. olive oil
1/2 t. salt
1/4 t. pepper

Whisk together all ingredients.

Panzanella Salad

Homestyle Baked Spaghetti

Everyone loves spaghetti and this baked version makes it ideal for toting to a potluck with friends.

8-oz. pkg. spaghetti, cooked
2 t. olive oil
1 c. favorite pasta sauce
1/4 lb. sliced mushrooms
1/2 c. green pepper, chopped
1/2 c. black olives, chopped
1/4 lb. mozzarella cheese, cubed
2 t. garlic, minced
1/2 t. Italian seasoning
1/2 t. seasoning salt
1/4 t. red pepper flakes
4 eggs
1/2 c. milk
3/4 c. sliced pepperoni
1/2 c. grated Parmesan cheese

Toss cooked spaghetti with oil in a large bowl; add sauce, mushrooms, green pepper, olives, mozzarella, garlic, seasonings and red pepper flakes. Mix well; spread in a lightly greased 13"x9" baking pan. Whisk together eggs and milk; pour over spaghetti mixture. Arrange pepperoni evenly on top; sprinkle with Parmesan. Bake at 375 degrees for 25 to 30 minutes, until bubbly and golden. Let stand for 5 minutes; cut into squares. Makes 6 to 8 servings.

Homestyle Baked Spaghetti

Shredded Chicken Sandwiches

Tender chicken piled high on a soft bun...just like the sandwiches from church socials or election day suppers.

4 T. olive oil
4 boneless, skinless chicken breasts
1 onion, chopped
10-3/4 oz. can cream of mushroom
　soup
1 c. chicken broth
2 t. soy sauce
2 t. Worcestershire sauce
1/2 c. sherry or chicken broth
salt and pepper to taste
8 multi-grain buns, split
Optional: pickle slices

Heat oil in a skillet over medium-high heat. Add chicken; brown for 5 minutes on each side. Arrange chicken in a slow cooker; set aside. Add onion to skillet; sauté until golden. Add remaining ingredients except buns to skillet; stir well and pour over chicken in slow cooker. Cover and cook on low setting for 6 to 8 hours. Shred chicken with a fork; spoon onto buns and garnish with pickles, if desired. Makes 8 sandwiches.

Shredded Chicken Sandwiches

Classic Tuna Noodle Casserole

One taste and it's easy to see why this was a regular on Mom's dinner table.

16-oz. pkg. wide egg noodles, cooked
2 10-3/4 oz. cans cream of mushroom
   soup
2 6-oz. cans tuna, drained
1 c. frozen peas, thawed
4-oz. can sliced mushrooms, drained
1 to 2 c. milk
salt and pepper to taste
8-oz. pkg. shredded Cheddar cheese
4 slices bread, toasted and cubed
1/4 c. butter, melted

Combine noodles, soup, tuna, peas and mushrooms; stir in enough milk to moisten well. Add salt and pepper to taste. Spread in a lightly greased 13"x9" baking pan; sprinkle with cheese and set aside. Toss together bread cubes and butter; sprinkle over top. Bake at 350 degrees for 25 minutes, until hot and bubbly. Serves 6.

Famous Broccoli Casserole

This casserole recipe is tried & true...we can't imagine any potluck without it!

16-oz. pkg. frozen broccoli
10-oz. pkg. frozen broccoli
2 10-3/4 oz. cans cream of chicken
   soup
16-oz. pkg. pasteurized process cheese
   spread, cubed
2 6.9-oz. pkgs. chicken-flavored rice
   vermicelli mix, prepared

Cook and drain broccoli; place in a slow cooker. Add soup and cheese; mix well. Stir in prepared rice vermicelli mix. Cover and cook on low setting for 3 to 4 hours, until hot and bubbly. Makes 32 servings.

sale

Cherry Delight Cobbler

No one can resist warm, fruit-filled cobbler. Spoon into bowls; then spoon on a little whipped cream for a real treat.

2 21-oz. cans cherry pie filling
3 pears, cored, peeled and chopped
1-1/4 c. all-purpose flour
1/4 c. plus 1 T. sugar, divided
1-1/2 t. baking powder
1/4 t. salt
1 c. whipping cream
2 T. sliced almonds

Blend together pie filling and pears in a greased 2-quart casserole dish; bake at 400 degrees for 15 minutes. In a large bowl, mix together flour, 1/4 cup sugar, baking powder and salt. Gradually stir in cream with a fork to form a thick, sticky batter. Remove casserole dish from oven; drop batter by spoonfuls on top of fruit mixture. Sprinkle with remaining sugar; top with almonds. Bake an additional 40 minutes at 400 degrees, until topping is golden. Makes 8 to 10 servings.

Chamomile Cooler

Garnish with fresh, edible chamomile flowers.

4 to 6 chamomile teabags
4 c. boiling water
12-oz. can frozen lemonade
    concentrate
2-1/2 c. ginger ale, chilled
Garnish: ice cubes

Steep teabags in boiling water for 10 minutes; discard teabags. When tea has cooled, combine with lemonade concentrate in a pitcher. Mix well; chill. At serving time, add ginger ale and ice cubes. Makes 8 servings.

If you have a variety of vintage linens for sale, display them on a clothesline...a terrific way to show off their one-of-a-kind patterns and colors.

county *fair*

Shiny Red Candy Apples

Jumbo Cinnamon Rolls

Hometown pride

and blue-ribbon best, late-summer celebrations that mean only one thing...it's county fair time! The fun is all in the sights & sounds...from the chatter along the midway to the dizzying rides on the Ferris wheel. But mostly, county fairs are all about the food!

Because the food is just too good to enjoy only once a year, we had to share with you some of our very favorite recipes you can easily make at home! Our Blue-Ribbon Chicken & Noodles are hearty and filled with plump noodles made from scratch. Shake-'Em-Up Lemonade is just like the frosty shake-ups you'll find at any fair booth. Bet you can't eat just one of our Jumbo Cinnamon Rolls or Prize-Winning Funnel Cakes...they are so yummy!

Why wait? Whip up a few of your favorites...you don't have to miss out on the sheer delight of fair food any time of year!

PRIZE-WINNING FUNNEL CAKES

SHINY RED CANDY APPLES

SUGARED CINNAMON PECANS

SHAKE-'EM-UP LEMONADE

ITALIAN SAUSAGES WITH PEPPERS & ONIONS

BLUE-RIBBON CHICKEN & NOODLES

FAMOUS FRIED CAULIFLOWER

TRAVELIN' TACOS

FIRST-PLACE APPLE DUMPLINGS

BEST-EVER SOFT PRETZELS

CRISPY, CRUNCHY KETTLE CORN

GIANT CREAM PUFFS

JUMBO CINNAMON ROLLS

117

county

Prize-Winning Funnel Cakes

The kid in all of us loves the powdered sugar topping! They are also delicious topped with your favorite fruit pie filling.

2 c. all-purpose flour
1 T. sugar
1 t. baking powder
1/4 t. salt
2 eggs, beaten
1-1/4 c. milk
oil for deep-frying
Garnish: powdered sugar
Optional: apple, cherry or
   blueberry pie filling

Sift together flour, sugar, baking powder and salt into a deep bowl. Make a well in the center; add eggs and enough milk to make a thin batter. Mix well. Heat several inches oil to 375 degrees in a deep saucepan. With fingertip over end of funnel, spoon batter by 1/2 cupfuls into a funnel over hot oil, one at a time, swirling funnel as batter is released. Cook until golden, about 2 minutes per side. Drain on paper towels. Sprinkle with powdered sugar; top with fruit pie filling if desired. Serve immediately. Makes about 4 servings.

Shiny Red Candy Apples

After coating the apples, quickly dip them into chopped nuts for an extra-special treat.

4 c. sugar
1 c. butter
1/4 c. white vinegar
1/4 c. boiling water
1/2 t. red food coloring
1/4 c. red cinnamon candies
10 lollipop sticks or wooden skewers
10 Granny Smith apples

Combine sugar, butter, vinegar, boiling water and food coloring in a large heavy metal saucepan. Cook over low heat until sugar dissolves. Increase heat to medium-high; boil without stirring for about 10 minutes, until mixture reaches hard-crack stage, or 290 to 310 degrees on a candy thermometer. Remove from heat; stir in cinnamon candies and let stand until bubbles subside. Insert sticks into apples. Dip apples into mixture; swirl to coat and dip into ice water to harden candy coating. Place on a lightly buttered baking pan until set. Store in a cool, dry place. Makes 10 apples.

fair

Sugared Cinnamon Pecans

One snack you can't put down! Serve 'em up in clear pastry bags or paper snow cone sleeves.

1 egg white
1/2 c. brown sugar, packed
1-1/2 t. vanilla extract
1 t. honey
1 t. cinnamon
2 c. pecan halves
Garnish: cinnamon-sugar

Line a baking sheet with wax paper; spray with non-stick cooking spray and set aside. In a medium bowl, beat egg white until very stiff with an electric mixer on high speed. Add brown sugar, vanilla, honey and cinnamon; stir until smooth. Add pecans; stir until well coated. Spread pecans in a single layer on prepared baking sheet. Bake at 300 degrees for 20 to 25 minutes, until golden. Immediately sprinkle pecans with cinnamon-sugar to coat. Remove from baking sheet; cool on a wire rack. Store in an airtight container. Makes 2 cups.

Shake-'Em-Up Lemonade

Who doesn't love the sweet and tangy taste of real lemonade? A tall glass is sure to beat the heat on any summer day!

1 lemon, halved
3 T. sugar
1-1/4 c. crushed ice
3 T. water

Squeeze juice from lemon halves into a 16-ounce shaker. Add sugar, enough ice to fill shaker 2/3 full and enough water to cover ice. Cover and shake until sugar dissolves. Pour over lemon halves in a tall glass. Makes one serving.

Fair food is perfect for kids' birthday parties! Send out invitations that resemble tickets from the ticket booth, then let the fun begin. A face-painting booth is a must, along with a ball or ring toss, basketball shooting and guessing the number of jelly beans in a jar. A day sure to be remembered!

Prize-Winning Funnel Cakes

Reward the blue-ribbon winners in your family...anytime! Prize-winning ribbons are a snap to make with fabric yo-yo's you can purchase from a fabric & craft store. Stitch lengths of ribbon to the back of each yo-yo and they're ready to hand out to the winners of the sack race or to Grandma for her famous apple pie.

Italian Sausages with Peppers & Onions

Toast the buns if you like...top with spicy mustard or a few shakes of hot sauce.

2 T. olive oil
2 red or green peppers, sliced
2 sweet onions, sliced
salt and pepper to taste
8 Italian sausages
8 hoagie buns, split and toasted

Heat oil on a large griddle over medium-high heat. Add peppers and onions in batches; cook until tender and dark golden. Add salt and pepper to taste; set aside, keeping warm. Place sausages on griddle; cook until well browned and cooked through. Serve sausages on buns, topped with peppers and onions. Serves 8.

Italian Sausages with
Peppers & Onions

Blue-Ribbon Chicken & Noodles

Just like the homestyle chicken & noodles you find being served up at the county fair church tent.

3 c. all-purpose flour
1 t. salt
5 eggs
1/2 t. yellow food coloring
2 T. white vinegar
3 to 4-lb. chicken
Optional: canned chicken broth,
   as needed

Thoroughly combine flour and salt in a large mixing bowl; make a well in the center and set aside. In a medium bowl, whisk together eggs and food coloring. Add vinegar and whisk again; pour into well in flour mixture. Work dough with hands until all ingredients are completely mixed. On a lightly floured surface, work dough until smooth, adding more flour if dough is sticky. Let dough rest for 20 minutes; divide in half. Roll out one portion of dough into a circle; continue to roll until thin (noodles will plump up when cooked). Cut dough into long strips, then cut crosswise to desired width.

Toss with flour to separate noodles. Set noodles aside and repeat with second portion of dough. Cover noodles loosely with paper towels and let dry for one to 2 hours, or overnight.

Place chicken in a 4-quart saucepan and cover with water. Bring to a boil; reduce heat and simmer until tender, about one hour. Reserving broth, remove chicken and let cool; remove meat from bone and set aside.

Measure reserved broth; add canned broth if necessary to equal 2 quarts. Bring broth to a boil. Drop noodles into broth a handful at a time, stirring constantly. Reduce heat to a simmer; cover and cook for 20 minutes, stirring occasionally to prevent sticking. Uncover and add reserved chicken. Cook, uncovered, an additional 20 minutes, or until noodles are tender, stirring occasionally. Makes 8 to 10 servings.

fair

Famous Fried Cauliflower

Harvest the bounty in your garden and fry other veggies like broccoli, eggplant, onion rings, green tomatoes or zucchini with the same batter. Try dill pickles (no need to steam first) or cheese that has been cut into sticks and frozen before coating with batter.

1 head cauliflower, cut into flowerets
2 c. all-purpose flour
1 T. salt
4 eggs
2 cloves garlic, pressed
1 T. fresh parsley, chopped
1 c. oil
Garnish: ranch salad dressing

Steam cauliflower just until fork-tender. Drain; rinse under cold water and drain again. Mix flour and salt in a shallow dish; set aside. Beat together eggs, garlic and parsley in a small bowl. Dip cauliflower into flour mixture, egg mixture and again in flour mixture, coating evenly. Heat oil in a large skillet over high heat for about 3 minutes. Place cauliflower in hot oil, a few pieces at a time, until golden on all sides. Drain on paper towels. Serve hot with salad dressing for dipping. Makes 6 to 8 servings.

Travelin' Tacos

Easy-to-eat tacos! Ideal for enjoying at the ballpark, during a football game or family picnic.

1 lb. ground beef
1-1/4 oz. pkg. taco seasoning mix
8 1-oz. pkgs. corn chips
2 c. lettuce, chopped
1 tomato, chopped
1/2 c. black olives, sliced
1 c. shredded Cheddar cheese
1/2 c. sour cream
1/2 c. salsa

Brown ground beef in a skillet over medium heat; drain. Stir in taco seasoning and prepare according to package directions. Gently crush corn chips inside unopened bags, then cut each bag open along one side edge. Spoon equal amounts of ground beef and remaining ingredients into each bag. Serve right in the bag with a fork. Makes 8 servings.

It's easy to enjoy county fair fun any time of year. Invite neighbors over for a pie bake-off or cake auction, and set up a spot in the backyard for kiddie tractor pulls...what a grand time!

First-Place Apple Dumplings

You'll win rave reviews when you serve these to family & friends. Top servings with big scoops of cinnamon ice cream... so yummy!

2 c. all-purpose flour
1/2 t. salt
2/3 c. shortening
2 to 3 T. cold water
6 tart apples, cored and peeled
1/2 c. sugar
1-1/2 t. cinnamon

Combine flour and salt in a medium bowl; cut in shortening to a cornmeal consistency. Stir in water. Roll out dough on a floured surface; cut into 6 squares large enough to cover apples. Set an apple in the center of each square. Mix together sugar and cinnamon; sprinkle over apples. Bring sides of dough together to cover apples; press to seal. Place seam-side down in a greased 13"x9" baking pan. Pour Cinnamon Syrup over dumplings. Bake at 500 degrees for 5 to 7 minutes. Reduce heat to 350 degrees; bake for an additional 35 to 40 minutes, until golden and apples are tender. Makes 6 dumplings.

Cinnamon Syrup:

2 c. water
1 c. sugar
4 t. butter
1/2 t. cinnamon

Combine ingredients in a small saucepan over medium heat; cook and stir until sugar dissolves.

Best-Ever Soft Pretzels

Enjoy these warm from the oven...there's nothing like them!

1 env. active dry yeast
1-1/2 c. very warm water (110 degrees)
1 T. sugar
2 t. salt
4 c. all-purpose flour
1 egg yolk
1 T. water
1/4 c. coarse salt

Dissolve yeast in warm water. Stir in sugar and salt until dissolved. Add flour; mix well. Turn onto floured board; knead for 5 minutes. Divide dough into 16 equal pieces. Roll into thin strips; shape into pretzels. Place on a well-greased baking sheet. Beat egg yolk with water; brush on pretzels. Sprinkle with salt; bake at 425 degrees for 15 to 20 minutes, until golden. Makes 16 pretzels.

Crispy, Crunchy Kettle Corn

Adding sugar turns plain popcorn into a sweet & salty fair favorite.

1/4 c. oil
1/2 c. popcorn, unpopped
1/4 c. sugar
1/2 to 1 t. salt

Place oil, popcorn and sugar in a large saucepan over medium heat. Cover pan tightly. Constantly shake pan back and forth as popcorn pops to avoid burning. When popping is complete, remove from heat. Sprinkle popcorn with salt. Makes about 6 to 8 servings.

Giant Cream Puffs

Watch everyone line up for one of the best old-fashioned sweet treats around! Cream puffs can also be filled with any flavor of ice cream, custard or pudding.

1 c. water
1/2 c. butter
1 c. all-purpose flour
1/4 t. salt
3 eggs
Garnish: powdered sugar or melted chocolate

Combine water and butter in a large heavy saucepan; bring to a boil. Remove from heat; stir until butter melts. Add flour and salt; mix thoroughly until dough comes away from sides of saucepan. Add eggs one at a time, beating well after each. Place dough in a pastry bag fitted with a large plain tip (or use a large spoon). Form 8 rounds on parchment paper-lined baking sheets; smooth tops with a finger dipped in cold water. Bake at 400 degrees for 30 to 35 minutes, until golden. Let stand for several minutes in oven with oven door open; cool on a wire rack. Slice puffs open; fill with Cream Filling. Garnish as desired with a sprinkle of powdered sugar or a drizzle of melted chocolate. Serve within one hour. Makes 8 puffs.

Cream Filling:

3-1/2 oz. pkg. instant French vanilla pudding mix
1 c. milk
1 c. whipping cream

In a medium bowl, beat pudding mix and milk together with an electric mixer on medium-high speed; set aside. In a separate bowl, beat whipping cream until soft peaks form. Gently fold whipped cream into pudding mixture. Chill.

fair

Jumbo Cinnamon Rolls

Whip up a batch of these ooey-gooey rolls for an unforgettable family treat.

1 c. very warm milk (110 degrees)
1 env. active dry yeast
1/2 c. sugar
2 eggs, beaten
1/3 c. margarine, melted and cooled
1 t. salt
4-1/2 c. all-purpose flour
3/4 c. brown sugar, packed
1/3 c. butter, softened
2-1/2 T. cinnamon

Combine milk, yeast and sugar in a large bowl; let stand for 10 minutes. Stir in eggs and margarine with a wooden spoon. Mix salt into flour; add flour to wet mixture one cup at a time until dough forms. Knead in bowl until smooth; place dough in a large bowl sprayed with non-stick vegetable spray. Cover; let rest until double in size. Generously spray a surface with non-stick vegetable spray; roll out dough into a 16"x21" rectangle. Spread with butter; combine brown sugar and cinnamon and sprinkle over top. Roll up dough and slice into 12 rolls; arrange in a lightly greased 13"x9" baking pan. Cover and let rise until nearly double in size, about 30 minutes. Bake rolls at 400 degrees until golden, about 15 minutes. Spread warm rolls with Vanilla Frosting; serve warm. Makes one dozen.

Vanilla Frosting:

3-oz. pkg. cream cheese, softened
1/4 c. butter, softened
1-1/2 c. powdered sugar
1/2 t. vanilla extract
1/8 t. salt

Beat together ingredients until smooth.

Serve up fair food in style! It's easy to find bright red and raincoat yellow squeeze bottles for catsup and mustard. Twirling spiral straws just seem to make sipping lemonade more fun and extra-tall, roomy paper cups can easily be filled with crispy French fries (don't forget the vinegar and catsup!)

bonfire

Sunset Skillet

Fireside Mulled Cider

Big Sky Muffins

Brisk autumn evenings...

and warm laughter combine to set the perfect stage for a gathering of friends. When the days become shorter, and we find the season has changed to "sweater weather," we love to celebrate with a bonfire party. This means hitching up a wagon to the tractor for an old-fashioned hayride, sliding apples onto long, metal skewers to be roasted later in the evening on the embers (then rolled in cinnamon-sugar...yum!) and keeping s'mores fixin's handy for an ooey-gooey late night treat.

A day spent in the crisp autumn air will kindle appetites, so by the time the sun begins to set and friends arrive, we make sure to have plenty of hearty food on hand. Mugs of Country Soup Supper served with Campfire Corn Dogs are sure to satisfy. Kids will love putting together their own Hobo Pouches and Loaded Potato Packets taste wonderful! Top off dinner with Chuck Wagon Cherry Pies or scrumptious Chocolate-Marshmallow Banana Boats.

So whether it's an autumn bonfire or backyard campout, now is the time to savor every moment of these golden days.

Chocolatey Spiced Coffee

This is a dreamy concoction for chocolate and coffee lovers.

1/2 c. ground coffee
5 c. water
1-1/2 t. cinnamon
1/2 t. nutmeg
1 c. milk
1/2 c. brown sugar, packed
1/3 c. chocolate syrup
1 t. vanilla extract
Optional: whipped cream

Brew coffee with water in a coffeemaker as usual, placing spices in filter with coffee. Set aside. Combine milk, sugar and syrup in a medium saucepan over low heat; cook and stir until sugar dissolves. Stir in brewed coffee and vanilla. Serve hot, garnished with dollops of whipped cream, if desired. Makes 6 servings.

Fireside Mulled Cider

The secret ingredients in this slow-cooker spiced cider are the fresh ginger and apple jelly.

3 qts. apple cider
1/2 c. apple jelly
1/4 t. nutmeg
2 4-inch by 1-inch strips orange peel
3 whole cloves
2 whole allspice
4-inch cinnamon stick
1/2-inch piece fresh ginger, peeled

Combine cider, jelly and nutmeg in a slow cooker; set aside. Place remaining ingredients in a square of doubled cheesecloth; bundle and tie with kitchen string. Place spice bag in slow cooker; cover and cook on high setting for 4 hours. Discard cheesecloth bag before serving. Makes 12 servings.

bonfire

Sunset Skillet

Cook this any way you like with sausage, diced ham or corned beef.

1 lb. ground pork sausage
2-1/2 c. potatoes, peeled and cubed
2 red peppers, diced
4 green onions, chopped
Optional: 1 to 2 T. oil
1-1/2 t. paprika
1-1/2 t. dried thyme
salt and pepper to taste
6 eggs
Garnish: chopped fresh parsley

In a large skillet over medium heat, cook sausage until browned. Drain sausage and set aside, leaving some drippings in skillet. Add potatoes, peppers and onions to skillet. Cook until potatoes are tender, crisp and golden, about 8 minutes, stirring frequently and adding oil to skillet if needed. Stir in sausage and seasonings. Make 6 wells in mixture with a spoon; break an egg into each. Reduce heat to low; cover and cook until eggs are cooked to desired doneness. Sprinkle with parsley. Serves 6.

Campfire Corn Dogs

An all-time favorite...corn dogs come out golden and delicious when prepared in a pie iron.

8-1/2 oz. pkg. corn muffin mix
8 to 10 hot dogs

Prepare corn muffin mix according to package directions; set aside. Place 3 hot dogs inside a well-greased cast iron hot dog cooker or a square pie iron. Pour in enough batter to fill the bottom of cooker. Close cooker; turn over and cook over a grill or campfire for 3 minutes. Turn over; cook for an additional 3 minutes, until cornbread is set. Repeat with remaining batter and hot dogs. Slice between hot dogs to serve. Makes 8 to 10 servings.

Fall evenings can be chilly, so keep plenty of wool blankets and throws on hand to cozy up around the fire. Bales of straw and old logs add extra seating. Put your wheelbarrow to work to help cart goodies from the house to the bonfire.

Country Soup Supper

Country Soup Supper

Hearty enough to stand alone, this soup is comforting with extraordinary flavor.

3 whole cloves
1 small yellow onion
5 15-1/2 oz. cans Great Northern
   beans, drained and rinsed
6 c. water
1/2 lb. cooked ham, diced, or 3 smoked
   ham hocks
2 c. potatoes, peeled and cubed
1-1/2 c. sweet onion, chopped
2/3 c. celery, chopped
2/3 c. carrot, peeled and sliced
1/2 t. dried thyme
1 t. dried parsley
1 bay leaf
1 t. salt
3/4 t. pepper
2 T. fresh parsley, chopped

Press cloves into whole onion; set aside. In a large stockpot, combine remaining ingredients except parsley; add onion with cloves. Bring to a boil; reduce heat, cover and simmer for 45 minutes, stirring occasionally. Discard onion with cloves and bay leaf. Remove ham hocks, if using; dice meat and return to soup. Stir in parsley. Makes 10 to 12 servings.

When serving soup, pull out your biggest soup or coffee mugs with handles, tie a bandanna on the handle for a lap-size napkin and slip a spoon into the knot...perfect!

Loaded Potato Packets

Top servings with sour cream and diced green onions...oh-so good!

3 baking potatoes, peeled and
    thinly sliced
1/2 onion, thinly sliced
1 T. garlic, minced
1/2 t. dried parsley
salt and pepper to taste
4 slices bacon, crisply cooked,
    crumbled and 1 T. drippings
    reserved
2 T. butter, sliced
1 c. shredded Cheddar cheese

Arrange potatoes on half of a lightly greased 30-inch length of heavy-duty aluminum foil. Top with onion; sprinkle with garlic, parsley, salt and pepper. Drizzle with reserved drippings, if desired; add butter, crumbled bacon and cheese. Fold aluminum foil loosely over potatoes; seal edges of packet tightly. Place on a baking sheet; bake at 350 degrees for 30 to 35 minutes. Open carefully and check for doneness; return to oven for a few minutes longer, if necessary. Makes 4 servings.

Hobo Pouches

The ingredients for this dinner travel well...just place in plastic zipping bags and toss in a cooler.

1-1/2 lbs. ground beef
1 t. Worcestershire sauce
1/2 t. seasoned pepper
1/8 t. garlic powder
3 redskin potatoes, sliced
1 onion, sliced
3 carrots, peeled and halved
olive oil and dried parsley to taste

Mix together ground beef, sauce, pepper and garlic powder; form into 4 to 6 patties. Place each patty on an 18-inch length of heavy-duty aluminum foil. Top patties with potatoes, onion and carrots; sprinkle with oil and parsley. Seal foil packets tightly and place on a baking sheet. Bake at 375 degrees for one hour. Makes 4 to 6 servings.

Keep in mind that eating outside means you'll need dinnerware strong enough to hold all the hearty food, but light enough to tote along. Vintage-style enamelware or graniteware does the trick...lightweight, but sturdy.

Big Sky Muffins

If you don't have a jumbo muffin tin handy, this recipe also makes 12 regular-size muffins. Follow the instructions below, baking at 400 degrees for 15 to 18 minutes, then cool for 5 minutes.

1-1/2 c. all-purpose flour
2 t. baking powder
1/4 t. baking soda
1/4 t. salt
1/4 c. shortening
8-oz. container sour cream
1/2 c. milk
1 egg, beaten
1/2 c. plus 2 T. sugar, divided
1/4 c. brown sugar, packed
1/4 c. chopped walnuts or pecans
1 t. cinnamon

Combine first 4 ingredients in a large bowl; mix well. Cut in shortening until mixture is crumbly; set aside. In a medium bowl, stir together sour cream, milk, egg and 1/2 cup sugar. Add to flour mixture and stir until just combined; set aside. Mix remaining sugar, brown sugar, nuts and cinnamon in a small bowl. Spoon half of batter into 6 greased jumbo 3-1/2" muffin cups; sprinkle with half the sugar mixture. Add remaining batter; sprinkle with remaining sugar mixture. Bake at 350 degrees for about 25 minutes, or until a toothpick tests clean. Cool on a wire rack for 15 minutes; serve warm. Makes 6 jumbo muffins.

Chuck Wagon Cherry Pies

With a pie iron, you can make a truly scrumptious dessert over the campfire.

21-oz. can cherry pie filling
1 t. almond extract
1 baked pound cake or angel food cake, sliced 1/2-inch thick
Garnish: softened butter, powdered sugar

Combine pie filling and extract in a small bowl; set aside. Spread cake slices lightly on one side with butter. Place one cake slice butter-side down in a cast iron pie iron; top with one to 2 tablespoons pie filling and a second cake slice, butter-side up. Close pie iron; cook over a grill or campfire until toasted and heated through, 4 to 6 minutes. Sprinkle pie with powdered sugar; repeat with remaining cake and pie filling. Makes 10 to 12 servings.

Chuck Wagon Cherry Pies

Gingerbread Cake in a Can

*Two favorite flavors pair up for this
yummy treat.*

2 empty, clean 29-oz. fruit cans or
   1-lb. coffee cans
14-1/2 oz. pkg. gingerbread cake mix
25-oz. jar cinnamon-flavored
   applesauce

Grease insides of cans; divide
applesauce between cans and set aside.
Prepare gingerbread mix according to
package directions; divide batter and
gently spoon into prepared cans.
Cover cans with aluminum foil; set
on a bed of hot coals. Check carefully
after about 15 minutes; gingerbread
should be raised and steaming. Re-cover
and continue cooking if necessary,
watching carefully (cake will be moist,
not fluffy). Remove from coals, leaving
a small vent open for steam to escape
if not ready to serve immediately. To
serve, spoon gingerbread into bowls;
top with warm applesauce. Makes
about 8 servings.

Chocolate-Marshmallow Banana Boats

*Gooey goodies…chocolate chips,
marshmallows and nuts inside a
grilled banana.*

4 bananas
6-oz. pkg. semi-sweet chocolate chips
10-1/2 oz. pkg. mini marshmallows
Optional: 1/2 c. peanuts, chopped

Pull back one section of peel on each
banana, without removing peel. Cut
a lengthwise wedge-shaped section
out of each banana; fill with chocolate
chips and marshmallows. Replace
peels; wrap each banana in aluminum
foil. Heat on a grill about 6 minutes,
until chips and marshmallows are
melted, or place on a baking sheet
and bake at 350 degrees for 7 to
10 minutes. Let cool slightly.
Makes 4 servings.

bonfire

Homemade Marshmallows

Unbelievably easy to make!

1-1/2 c. water, divided
4 envs. unflavored gelatin
3 c. sugar
1-1/4 c. light corn syrup
1/4 t. salt
2 t. vanilla extract
1-1/2 c. powdered sugar, divided

Spray a 13"x9" baking pan with non-stick vegetable spray. Line with wax paper; coat wax paper with non-stick vegetable spray and set aside. Pour 3/4 cup water into a medium bowl and sprinkle gelatin over top; let stand 5 minutes. Place sugar, corn syrup, remaining water, salt and vanilla in a heavy saucepan; bring to a boil. Cook over high heat for about 9 minutes until mixture reaches the soft-ball stage, 234 to 243 degrees on a candy thermometer. Beat hot mixture slowly into gelatin mixture for about 10 minutes, or until very stiff. Pour into prepared pan; smooth top with a spatula. Let stand overnight,

uncovered, until firm. Invert baking pan onto a surface covered with one cup powdered sugar; peel off wax paper. Cut into squares with a knife; roll in remaining powdered sugar to coat. Makes about 2 dozen.

A wooden tool caddy lined with parchment paper makes a whimsical s'mores carrier...just fill with marshmallows, chocolate bars, graham crackers and cookies.

For fun, try a fresh twist on this campfire classic...
- *Use chocolate or cinnamon-flavored graham crackers.*
- *Top graham crackers with peanut butter and fruit jam before adding toasted marshmallows.*
- *Enjoy any of your favorite candy bars...a peanut butter cup or peppermint patty...scrumptious!*
- *Layer on thinly sliced bananas or apples...yummy with melted chocolate.*

gifts
for
giving

Chocolatey Gingerbread Cut-Out Cookies

Ho-Ho Snowballs

Swirled Peppermint Bark

Handmade gifts...

those made with your heart as well as your hands, are always the ones we treasure most. Made with love, these gifts hold a special place in our hearts. Sweet family photos, vintage ornaments, tiny stockings or mittens and a snowy dusting of glitter lend a sentimental feel to a Christmas Memory Wreath. Mismatched teacups, along with old-fashioned jelly jars and glass measuring cups, are easily filled to become charming Candle Gifts.

Tasty gifts from your kitchen are sure to be welcome too. No one can resist Ho-Ho Snowballs or Chocolate-Dipped Marshmallows...they're scrumptious! Top off gift bags with Clothespin Clips and tuck gift cards into clever Pocket Tags...we'll show you how easy they are to make.

Call your best girlfriends, whip up some easy appetizers and spend the afternoon creating these gifts. Not only will you make some wonderful memories together, you'll be giving a gift that's a part of yourself. What could be sweeter?

Chocolatey Gingerbread Cut-Out Cookies

Try this chocolatey version of everyone's favorite cut-out cookie.

1-1/2 c. semi-sweet chocolate chips
2-3/4 c. all-purpose flour
1 t. baking soda
1/2 t. salt
1/2 t. ground ginger
1/2 t. cinnamon
3 T. butter, softened
3 T. sugar
1/2 c. molasses
1/4 c. water
Optional: colored icing, candy sprinkles

Place chocolate chips in a microwave-safe bowl. Microwave on high setting for one minute; stir. Microwave an additional 10 to 15 seconds, if needed. Stir; cool to room temperature. Combine flour, baking soda, salt and spices in a medium bowl; set aside. Blend together butter and sugar in a small bowl until creamy; beat in melted chocolate and molasses. Gradually add flour mixture alternately with water; beat until smooth. Gather dough into a ball; pack firmly, cover and chill for one hour. Working with half of dough at a time, roll out 1/4-inch thick on a floured surface. Cut with cookie cutters as desired; place on ungreased baking sheets. Bake at 350 degrees for 5 to 6 minutes, until edges are set and centers are still soft. Cool on baking sheets for 2 minutes; remove to wire racks to finish cooling. Decorate with icing and sprinkles, if desired. Makes 2-1/2 to 3 dozen cookies.

for giving

Swirled Peppermint Bark

Swirls of white and semi-sweet chocolate!

8-oz. pkg. semi-sweet baking chocolate
   squares, chopped
6-oz. pkg. white baking chocolate
   squares, chopped
Optional: 1/2 t. peppermint extract
1/2 c. peppermint candy canes, crushed

Place chocolates in 2 separate microwave-safe bowls. Working with one bowl at a time, microwave on high setting for one minute; stir until smooth. Microwave an additional 10 to 15 seconds, if needed. Pour semi-sweet chocolate onto a wax paper-lined baking sheet; set aside. Stir extract into white chocolate, if using. Slowly pour white chocolate over semi-sweet chocolate on baking sheet. Swirl chocolates together with a knife; sprinkle with crushed candy. Chill until firm, about one hour. Use wax paper to lift bark from baking sheet; break into pieces. Store tightly covered at room temperature. Makes about one pound.

Ho-Ho Snowballs

Show off these pretty treats arranged inside a glass apothecary jar.

2 6-oz. pkgs. white chocolate chips
1/4 c. heavy cream
2 T. bourbon or heavy cream
6-oz. pkg. slivered almonds, very finely
   ground
1-1/2 c. sweetened flaked coconut

Place chocolate chips and cream in a medium bowl set over a pan of hot (not boiling) water; stir until melted and smooth. Stir in bourbon or cream and almonds. Spread in a lightly greased 8"x8" baking pan. Chill for about one hour, until firm. Cut into one-inch squares; roll each square into a ball, then roll in coconut. Keep chilled. Makes about 5 dozen.

Pipe cleaners make fun, old-fashioned toppers for packaged cookies and candies. Twist together one red and one white pipe cleaner, then bend the top over to resemble a candy cane...sweet and simple!

Gumdrop Jar

Fill a regular, quart-size Mason jar with gumdrops and slip an oyster votive holder inside the top of the jar…it will be a perfect fit. Add a votive candle to the holder, and top off the jar with a bow. Or, instead of using gumdrops, you could place sprigs of evergreen inside the jar and dust with mica snow…so sparkly!

Pocket Tags

Pretty papers and scrapbook add-ons are ideal for a one-of-a-kind tag that holds a surprise gift card inside! Use your imagination…add a zig-zag machine stitch to create a pocket for holding the gift card, or simply glue a pocket in place. Add a trim of rick rack, twill tape, ribbon or buttons to finish your tag with whimsy.

Clothespin Clips

With just a few basics, you can make these charming clothespins! Just right for keeping appointment cards clipped to calendars, as placecard holders (clip to the edges of plates), or to secure a cello bag filled with goodies.

Using a small foam brush, apply a thin layer of découpage medium to one side of a clothespin. Lay clothespin glue-side down onto scrapbook paper and press firmly. Turn clip and paper over to smooth out any wrinkles; turn back over to lay flat and dry. Once dry, use a craft knife to trim around the edges of the clothespin.

Using the same foam brush, apply a topcoat of découpage medium over the scrapbook-papered top of the clothespin to seal; let dry completely.

Pocket Tags

Chocolate Lovers' Dream Cookies

Picture P 155

A minty filling and a chocolate glaze combine to make an absolutely delectable sandwich cookie.

1 c. butter, softened
1 c. sugar
1/2 c. brown sugar, packed
2/3 c. baking cocoa
1-1/2 t. baking powder
1/4 t. baking soda
3 eggs
2 t. vanilla extract
2 c. all-purpose flour

In a large bowl, with an electric mixer on low speed, blend butter, sugars, cocoa, baking powder and baking soda. Add eggs and vanilla. Beat in as much flour as possible; stir in any remaining flour. Cover; chill at least 2 hours. Form into 1-1/2 inch balls; place 2 inches apart on ungreased baking sheet. Bake at 375 degrees for 8 to 10 minutes. Let stand one minute on baking sheet; remove to wire racks to cool. Spread filling on flat side of half the cookies; press on remaining cookies to make sandwiches. Spread tops with glaze; place on a wire rack until glaze sets. Wrap each sandwich in plastic wrap. Keep chilled. Makes 1-1/2 dozen.

gifts

Filling:

1/3 c. butter, softened
3 T. green crème de menthe
4 c. powdered sugar

Mix butter and crème de menthe in a medium bowl. With an electric mixer on low speed, gradually beat in powdered sugar, adding a little more crème de menthe if necessary until spreadable.

Glaze:

6 1-oz. sqs. semi-sweet baking
    chocolate, chopped
1/3 c. whipping cream

Cook and stir chocolate and cream in a medium saucepan over low heat until melted. Remove from heat; let stand 20 minutes, until slightly thickened.

for giving

Cowboy Cookies Jar Mix

When it comes to jar mixes, we recommend using a wooden tamper. It's not only the easiest way to layer the ingredients, but the best way to make sure they all fit nicely inside the jar.

1-1/3 c. all-purpose flour
1 t. baking powder
1 t. baking soda
1/2 c. brown sugar, packed
1 t. cinnamon
1/2 c. sugar
1-1/3 c. long-cooking oats, uncooked
1 c. semi-sweet chocolate chips
1/2 c. chopped pecans, toasted
1 c. sweetened flaked coconut

Mix flour, baking powder and baking soda. Place in a one-quart, wide-mouth canning jar; press down firmly to pack. Mix brown sugar and cinnamon; add to jar and press down firmly. Layer remaining ingredients in order given, pressing down firmly after each layer (jar will be very full). Seal tightly; attach instructions.

Instructions:

Combine 1/2 cup softened butter, 2 eggs, one teaspoon vanilla extract and cookie mix in a large bowl; mix well. Form into walnut-size balls; place 2 inches apart on greased baking sheets. Bake at 350 degrees for 11 to 15 minutes, until edges are lightly golden. Cool on wire racks. Makes 4 dozen cookies.

Recycle vintage style cards and stamps into gift tags. Trimmed with decorative-edged scissors and tied on a package of goodies, they're pretty enough to be gifts by themselves.

*Christmas Memory
Wreath*

Christmas Memory Wreath

Sweet cards, vintage ornaments and sentimental photos too special to be tucked away are a delight all season long when they become part of this heartfelt wreath.

Sparkly pipe cleaners are used to wire on ornaments, tiny stockings and glittery greetings. Photocopies of favorite photos are trimmed with decorative-edged scissors, then arranged on pretty paper using spray adhesive. Be sure to let the adhesive dry 3 to 5 minutes before arranging the photo just in case you want to loosen and rearrange the photo. For extra sparkle, lightly spray photo corners or edges with spray adhesive and dust with glitter.

S'mores Kit with
Snow Cocoa Recipe

Old-fashioned ornament boxes, vintage picnic tins, dainty teacups, tall Mason jars and charming tea towels...all are clever containers to tuck your homemade cookies and confections into. Just add an evergreen or berry sprig, a length of rick rack, ribbon or Christmasy clothespin clip, and your treats are dressed up and ready for gift giving!

Snow Cocoa

Big and little kids will love getting a S'mores Kit, and it's so simple to put together. Arrange packages of graham crackers, marshmallows and chocolate bars inside a cheery enamelware pail. Be sure to slip in our recipe for Snow Cocoa too. Made in a slow cooker, this creamy white cocoa is ready for everyone to enjoy after their frosty outdoor fun!

2 c. whipping cream
6 c. milk
1 t. vanilla extract
12-oz. pkg. white chocolate chips

Combine all ingredients in a slow cooker. Cover and cook on low setting for 2 to 2-1/2 hours, or until chocolate is melted and mixture is hot. Stir well to combine before serving. Makes 10 servings.

Merry Magnets

Oh-so simple! Remove the backing from self-adhesive clear page pebbles and arrange on decorative paper. Trim around the pebbles and use craft glue to secure a magnet button to the back of each pebble. Set aside to let glue dry. If you have glass pebbles, use them too...just add glue to the back of the pebble and place directly on decorative paper. Set aside to dry...the glue will dry clear. Then trim paper with a craft knife and glue on a button magnet. Have fun with your magnets...glue button magnets to the backs of flat-back buttons, metal bottle caps or vintage-style typewriter keys for terrific monogram magnets!

Candle Gifts

Flickering candlelight is so pretty, and with just a few basic supplies, it's easy to make your own handpoured candles.

There are lots of books and internet sites available that will get you started with a supply list and all the basics of beginning.

Once you've read up on all the how-to's and are ready to start, look for clever containers for your candles. Heat-resistant, vintage-style containers such as jelly jars, glass measuring cups, glass molds, metal jelly molds and teacups would all be terrific. To give your candles a little sparkle, once you've filled your container with wax, lightly dust the top with mica snow.

148   *Merry Magnets*   *Candle Gifts*

Holiday Tray

It's simple to turn a practical gift into a treasured one. Coat a wooden tray with acrylic paint; let dry and repeat with a second coat if needed. Apply spray adhesive to secure copies of photos, tags, stamps, ticket stubs, ribbon or other embellishments inside the tray. Use a foam brush to spread découpage medium over all items inside the tray; dust lightly with glitter while still wet. Let dry completely.

You can also arrange photos, ticket stubs and recipe cards on a tray, then top with a piece of acrylic plastic. Acrylic plastic is easily found at your hardware store...just ask to

have it cut to fit your tray. Then, when you want to change your design, it's easy to lift the plastic and rearrange the items.

Toffee Brownie Bites

These brownies are anything but ordinary!

4 1-oz. sqs. unsweetened
   baking chocolate
1 c. butter
2 c. sugar
4 eggs
2 t. vanilla extract
1-1/2 c. all-purpose flour
1/2 t. salt
1/2 c. chopped pecans
1/2 c. toffee baking bits

Melt chocolate and butter in a medium saucepan over low heat; stir until smooth. Cool for 5 minutes. Combine chocolate mixture, sugar, eggs and vanilla in a large bowl; beat for one minute with an electric mixer on high speed. Beat in flour and salt on low speed for 30 seconds; beat on medium speed for one minute. Spread half of batter in a 13"x9" baking pan that has been greased on the bottom only. Spread filling over top; carefully spread remaining batter over filling. Gently swirl through layers with a knife to marble; sprinkle with nuts and toffee. Bake at 350 degrees for 45 to 50 minutes, or until a toothpick tests clean. Cool completely on a wire rack. Cut into small squares; keep chilled. Makes 3 to 4 dozen.

Filling:

2 8-oz. pkgs. cream cheese, softened
1/2 c. sugar
1 egg
2 t. vanilla extract
1/2 c. chopped pecans
1/2 c. toffee baking bits

Beat cream cheese, sugar, egg and vanilla with an electric mixer on high speed until smooth. Stir in nuts and toffee.

for giving

Marshmallow-Chocolate Fudge

Everyone loves fudge, but with double the chocolate, this recipe is one you'll be asked to share!

2-1/2 c. sugar
1/4 c. butter
5-oz. can evaporated milk
3/4 t. salt
7-oz. jar marshmallow creme
1 c. semi-sweet chocolate chips
1 c. milk or dark chocolate chips
3/4 t. vanilla extract
Optional: 1/2 c. chopped walnuts

Line a 9"x9" baking pan with aluminum foil; grease lightly and set aside. Combine sugar, butter, evaporated milk and salt in a large heavy saucepan. Cook over medium heat until sugar dissolves, stirring occasionally; bring to a full rolling boil. Reduce heat slightly. Boil, stirring constantly, for 5 minutes. Remove from heat. Add marshmallow creme, chocolate chips and vanilla; beat until well mixed. Stir in nuts, if using. Spread in prepared pan; chill for 2 to 3 hours, until firm. Lift fudge from pan; peel off foil and cut into squares. Makes about 2-1/2 pounds.

Variation:

Peanut Butter Fudge:

Instead of 2 cups chocolate chips, use one cup peanut butter chips plus one cup creamy peanut butter. Replace walnuts with peanuts, if desired.

Wrap up a yummy cocoa gift in no time! Along with your favorite cocoa mix, give lots of candy stir-ins...mini candy bars, candy-coated chocolates, peanut butter cups, malted milk balls and chocolate drops. Melting a candy bar in warm cocoa turns it into something absolutely amazing!

Cranberry Margaritas

One sip reveals a tart & tangy twist to a classic recipe.

10 T. tequila
10 T. frozen cranberry juice cocktail
    concentrate, thawed
1/2 c. jellied cranberry sauce
5 T. lime juice
3 T. orange liqueur
3-1/2 c. ice cubes, divided
Garnish: red sanding sugar, coarse salt

Mix all ingredients except ice cubes and garnish in a blender; blend until smooth. Add ice cubes; blend until slushy and set aside. Mix sugar and salt in a saucer. Dampen rims of 6 margarita glasses and press into sugar mixture. Fill glasses carefully. Makes 6 servings.

Cranberry Margaritas

Chocolate Martinis

*Cowboy Cookies
Jar Mix*

Chocolate Martinis

Chocolate in a whole new light.

3/4 c. hard-shell chocolate ice cream
    coating
1 c. chocolate liqueur
3/4 c. half-and-half
1/4 c. vodka
2 c. ice cubes
Optional: whipped cream, chocolate
    shavings

Pour chocolate coating into a saucer.
Dip the rims of 4 to 6 chilled martini
glasses in coating; chill until set.
Combine liqueur, half-and-half and
vodka in a pitcher; set aside. Working
in batches, fill a martini shaker with
ice cubes; add liqueur mixture and
shake. Strain into prepared glasses.
Garnish as desired. Makes 4 to
6 servings.

Chocolate-Dipped Marshmallows

The kids will love making these with you!

1 c. semi-sweet or white chocolate
    chips
2 t. oil
10-oz. pkg. marshmallows
Garnish: mini candy-coated chocolates,
    candy sprinkles

Combine chocolate chips and oil in
a microwave-safe bowl. Microwave
on medium setting for one to
1-1/2 minutes until chocolate is
softened; stir until smooth. With a
candy dipping tool or toothpick,
dip marshmallows into chocolate to
cover completely. Sprinkle with
desired garnish; set on wax paper
until firm. Makes about 3 dozen.

*Marshmallow-Chocolate Fudge
and Peanut Butter Fudge*

*Chocolate-Dipped
Marshmallows*

Sweet & Salty Pretzel Snacks

Try using ring-shaped pretzels and your favorite flavor of chocolate drops...you just can't go wrong.

48 waffle-shaped mini pretzels
8-oz. pkg. striped milk chocolate
   drops, unwrapped
1/4 c. red and green candy-coated
   chocolates

Place pretzels on a parchment paper-lined baking sheet. Top each with a chocolate drop. Bake at 170 degrees for 4 to 6 minutes, until chocolate is softened. Quickly press a candy-coated chocolate in the center of each pretzel. Cool for a few minutes; chill for 10 minutes, until set. Store in plastic zipping bags. Makes 4 dozen.

Sweet Nibbles

These sweet little mice will be welcome in any home! For white mice, simply substitute white milk chocolate drops and white chocolate chips.

6-oz. pkg. semi-sweet chocolate chips
2 t. shortening
24 maraschino cherries with stems,
   well drained
24 milk chocolate drops
48 almond slices
Garnish: white and red gel icing

Melt chocolate chips and shortening in a double boiler over low heat; stir until smooth. To make each mouse, hold a cherry by the stem and dip into melted chocolate. Set on wax paper; press a chocolate drop onto opposite side of cherry from stem. For ears, insert 2 almond slices between cherry and chocolate drop. For eyes, pipe 2 white icing dots with red icing centers. Cover; keep refrigerated. Makes 2 dozen.

Sweet & Salty Pretzel Snacks

Sweet Nibbles

Cranberry-Orange Loaf

Tangy cranberries, sweet apricots and citrusy orange flavors blend together in this delicious quick bread.

2 c. all-purpose flour
1 c. sugar
2 t. baking powder
1/2 t. salt
1 t. orange zest
2 eggs, beaten
1/2 c. milk
1/2 c. butter, melted
3/4 c. cranberries, coarsely chopped
3/4 c. chopped walnuts, toasted
1/2 c. dried apricots, chopped

In a large bowl, stir together flour, sugar, baking powder, salt and zest. Make a well in the center; set aside. In a medium bowl, stir together eggs, milk and butter; add to flour mixture. Stir just until moistened; fold in cranberries, nuts and apricots. Spread in an 8"x4" loaf pan that has been greased on bottom and 1/2 inch up sides. Bake at 350 degrees for 65 to 70 minutes, until a toothpick tests clean. Cover with aluminum foil during last 20 minutes of baking time. Cool in pan on a wire rack for 10 minutes; invert onto rack and cool completely. Makes one loaf.

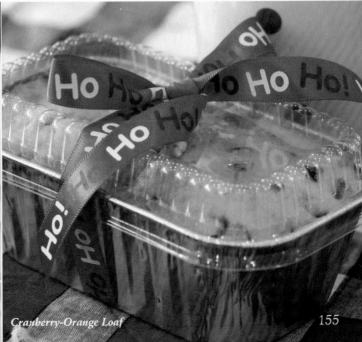

Chocolate Lovers' Dream Cookies   *Cranberry-Orange Loaf*

DESSERTS

Celebration Cupcake Cones, 66
Cherry Delight Cobbler, 115
Chocolate-Marshmallow Banana Boats, 136
Chuck Wagon Cherry Pies, 134
Crispy, Crunchy Kettle Corn, 125
Crustless Pumpkin Pie, 32
Dreamy Chocolate Pecan Pie, 42
First-Place Apple Dumplings, 124
Giant Cream Puffs, 126
Gingerbread Cake in a Can, 136
Golden Tequila Lime Tart, 105
Hokey-Pokey Cupcakes, 67
Luscious Lemon Layer Cake, 70
Marbled Pumpkin Cheesecake, 31
Mile-High Chocolate Meringue Pie, 63
Mom's Apple-Cranberry Pie, 33
Mom's Lemon Icebox Pie, 89
Nutty Popcorn Snack Mix, 20
Old-Fashioned Gingerbread Torte, 45
Old-Fashioned Vanilla Ice Cream, 88
Pineapple Upside-Down Cake, 62
Prize-Winning Funnel Cakes, 118
Pumpkin Ice Cream, 17
Shiny Red Candy Apples, 118
Spooky Spiderweb Cupcakes, 18
Sugared Cinnamon Pecans, 119
Summertime Strawberry Shortcake, 90
Sweet Success Trail Mix, 71
Triple-Delight German Chocolate Cake, 68
Very Berry Peach Pie, 91

MAINS

BBQ Nachos, 108
Blue-Ribbon Chicken & Noodles, 122
Brie-Stuffed Burgers, 86
Campfire Corn Dogs, 131
Classic Tuna Noodle Casserole, 114
Country-Style Baby Back Ribs, 87
Cranberry-Apple Glazed Turkey, 29
Golden Crab Cakes, 101
Golden Shepherd's Pie, 34
Grilled Salmon Quesadillas with Roasted Corn Salsa, 102
Hobo Pouches, 133
Homestyle Baked Spaghetti, 112
Italian Sausages with Peppers & Onions, 120
Mummy Hot Dogs, 14
Pineapple-Honey Glazed Ham, 38
Pork Chops with Herbed Stuffing, 58
Roast Turkey with Herb Butter, 28
Shredded Chicken Sandwiches, 113
Smokey Bacon-Gouda Burgers, 84
Travelin' Tacos, 123

SALADS

Country-Style 3-Bean Salad, 56
Crunchy Apple-Pear Salad, 24
Crunchy Hot Chicken Salad, 12
Dilly Blue Cheese Potato Salad, 82
Frosty Fruit Salad, 109
Grandma's Gelatin Salad, 40
Greek Pasta Salad, 83
Grilled Corn & Shrimp Salad, 97
Minted Asparagus Slaw, 98
Overnight Layered Salad, 54
Panzanella Salad, 110
Sweet Ambrosia Salad, 56
Tangy Turkey Cobb Salad, 34
Zesty Apple Slaw, 83

SIDES

Brown Sugar-Glazed Carrots, 57
Buttery Scalloped Potatoes, 57
Calico Beans, 82
Dandy Deviled Eggs, 59
Famous Broccoli Casserole, 114
Famous Fried Cauliflower, 123
Fried Green Tomatoes with Roasted Red Pepper Sauce, 96
Garlicky Parmesan Asparagus, 30
Grilled Sweet Corn with Lime-Chive Butter, 80
Loaded Potato Packets, 133

U.S. to Canadian Recipe Equivalents

Volume Measurements

1/4 teaspoon	1 mL
1/2 teaspoon	2 mL
1 teaspoon	5 mL
1 tablespoon = 3 teaspoons	15 mL
2 tablespoons = 1 fluid ounce	30 mL
1/4 cup	60 mL
1/3 cup	75 mL
1/2 cup = 4 fluid ounces	125 mL
1 cup = 8 fluid ounces	250 mL
2 cups = 1 pint	500 mL
= 16 fluid ounces	
4 cups = 1 quart	1 L

Weights

1 ounce	30 g
4 ounces	120 g
8 ounces	225 g
16 ounces = 1 pound	450 g

Oven Temperatures

300° F	150° C
325° F	160° C
350° F	180° C
375° F	190° C
400° F	200° C
450° F	230° C

Baking Pan Sizes

SQUARE		LOAF	
8x8x2 inches	2 L = 20x20x5 cm	9x5x3 inches	2 L = 23x13x7 cm
9x9x2 inches	2.5 L = 23x23x5 cm	ROUND	
RECTANGULAR		8x1-1/2 inches	1.2 L = 20x4 cm
13x9x2 inches	3.5 L = 33x23x5 cm	9x1-1/2 inches	1.5 L = 23x4 cm